D1300544

Novenas

Other Loyola Press books
edited by William G. Storey

**A Prayer Book of Catholic Devotions:
Praying the Seasons and Feasts of the Church Year**

Novenas

*Prayers of Intercession
and Devotion*

edited by William G. Storey

LOYOLAPRESS.

CHICAGO

LoyolaPress.

3441 N. Ashland Avenue
Chicago, Illinois 60657
(800) 621-1008
WWW.LOYOLABOOKS.ORG

© 2007 William G. Storey
All rights reserved

Nihil Obstat
Reverend William H. Woestman, OMI, JCD
Censor Deputatus
March 4, 2007

Imprimatur
Reverend George J. Rassas
Vicar General
Archdiocese of Chicago
March 8, 2007

The *Nihil Obstat* and *Imprimatur* are official declarations that a book is free of doctrinal and moral error. No implication is contained therein that those who have granted the *Nihil Obstat* and *Imprimatur* agree with the content, opinions, or statements expressed. Nor do they assume any legal responsibility associated with publication.

Unless otherwise noted, the Scripture quotations contained herein are from the *New Revised Standard Version of the Bible* © 1989 Division of Christian Education of the National Council of Churches of Christ in the U.S.A. and are used by permission. All rights reserved.

Scripture passages cited as "TEV" are taken from *Today's English Version of the Bible: Good News Bible* (New York: American Bible Society, 1976, 1979).

Unless otherwise noted, psalms are taken from *Psalms for Praise and Worship: A Complete Liturgical Psalter* edited and prepared by John C. Holbert (Nashville: Abingdon Press, 1992).

Psalm passages cited as "Grail" are taken from *The Psalms: Grail Translation from the Hebrew* © 1993 by the Ladies of the Grail (England). Used by permission of GIA Publications, Inc., exclusive agent. All rights reserved.

Acknowledgments continue on page 265.

Interior design by Donna Antkowiak

Library of Congress Cataloging-in-Publication Data
Novenas : prayers of intercession and devotion / edited by William G. Storey.
     p. cm.
  Includes bibliographical references and index.
  ISBN 978-0-8294-2161-3 (alk. paper)
  1. Novenas. I. Storey, William George, 1923–
BX2170.N7N69 2007
242'.802—cd22

                              2007007882

Printed in China
07 08 09 10 IMG 10 9 8 7 6 5 4 3 2

For Bert Ghezzi.

Contents

Novenas to the Saints   113

Novenas for Special Occasions   197

Litanies and Insistent Prayer   245

Introduction

When I was teaching at the preparatory school in St. Michael's College School in Toronto, Ontario, I used to attend the novena to Our Lady of Perpetual Help each week. The novena was held in a Redemptorist church several times throughout the day, and was closed each time with Benediction of the Blessed Sacrament.

Why did I go regularly? To pray for my success in teaching large classes of adolescent boys, to pray for the conversion of my parents, to pray for my own fuller conversion, to pray about what I was going to do with my life, to pray for my own special friends and for the welfare of the Church. It was also a good place to go to confession since the confessionals were available at the same hours as the novena.

On reflection, I think I also attended the novena because it gave me a fresh vision of popular Catholicism. At the time, the Latin mass was a rather drab affair in most parishes: encased in Latin, little or no music, muttered, and with only minimal participation by the congregation. On the other hand, the novena was a popular experience: well and freely attended; with organ music, singing, expressive intercessory prayer in English, lights, and incense; and focused on the miraculous icon of our Lady and on Jesus in the Blessed Sacrament.

Such a vital experience led me to appreciate the duty and privilege of intercessory prayer in my life.

Of course, I already knew something about Jesus' prayer life in the synagogue, the temple, on the lonely mountainsides of Galilee, and during the star-studded night—but I did not have a good appreciation of intercessory prayer or the role of God's Mother until I had frequented the novena of Our Lady of Perpetual Help. The great cross section of praying people I encountered each week at the novena drove home the value and necessity of prayer for all human needs. It helped me to understand better how Jesus taught us to pray and how he gave us a model prayer to help us comprehend the main themes of our own.

Jesus himself called on God as "Abba, [dear] Father" (Mark 14:36) and taught us to use the same invocation to begin the Lord's Prayer. After teaching us to call upon God as Abba, Jesus shows us the order of prayer. First comes the hallowing of God's name, the coming of the reign of God, and the doing of God's will—on earth as it is in heaven. Then the prayer encourages us to pray for our daily bread (physical and spiritual), for the forgiveness of our sins, and for deliverance from all trials and tribulations.

In the end, I found novenas and triduums to be concrete expressions of the second half of the Lord's Prayer. We are, of course, always praying implicitly for the earlier intentions, but we express our personal and communal needs more explicitly in the later ones.

Novenas

A novena is nine days of concentrated prayer. The nine days recall the nine days of prayer observed in the upper room by Mary, the apostles, and other disciples of Jesus between Ascension Thursday and Pentecost Sunday (Acts 1:12–14). These crucial nine days before the gift of the Spirit set the pattern for nine days of special prayer on other occasions and for other needs.

For centuries novenas have been celebrated publicly to prepare for outstanding feasts like Christmas and Pentecost and to remember our dead for nine days after their demise. Many people also have recourse to private novenas in the family or by themselves. They are often held as preparations for feasts and name days and as prayers of petition for special needs. One of the most famous annual novenas in the western hemisphere, to Our Lady of Guadalupe, Mother of the Americas, is celebrated each year in churches, homes, and neighborhoods to prepare for December 12.

Some parishes and downtown churches hold the so-called perpetual, or continuous, novenas to Our Lady of Guadalupe, Our Lady of Perpetual Help, the Mother of Sorrows, Our Lady of the Rosary, St. Joseph, St. Anthony, St. Jude, and many others. These are held on a given day of the week, all year long, so that people can begin a novena of nine weeks anytime they wish. In churches, the more popular the novena the more often it is held on the day set aside for it.

In addition to novenas of petition, there are also novenas of thanksgiving for favors received; novenas in time of special difficulty; novenas for the sick, the dying, and the faithful departed; and so forth.

Triduums

Triduums are held for similar reasons. A triduum is a three-day observance of concentrated prayer, public or private, originating from the three days of the Easter Triduum, so central to celebrating the paschal mystery in the Liturgy of Holy Week.

Praying in the Spirit

By praying, one is essentially joining the indwelling Holy Spirit, who "helps us in our weakness; for we do not know how to pray as we ought, but that very Spirit intercedes with sighs too deep for words. And God, who searches the heart, knows what is the mind of the Spirit, because the Spirit intercedes for the saints according to the will of God" (Romans 8:26–27).

At our Baptism we Christians are infused with the Holy Spirit, who continually lives in us and prays for us to the heavenly Father—"God has sent the Spirit of his Son into our hearts, crying, 'Abba! Father!'" (Galatians 4:6). Unless we thwart it by serious sin, the unceasing prayer of the Spirit continues without interruption for our entire lifetime. If we have the misfortune to lose the gift of the Spirit, its restoration is immediate when we repent and seek absolution in the sacrament of Reconciliation. Moreover, the Spirit moves us to use the traditional prayers of the Catholic religion that are contained in the Holy Liturgy and in the popular devotions that flourish in our midst. These are gifts of God for the people of God and a school of prayer from childhood to old age.

To pray well, therefore, we need to be *aware* of the divine presence in our hearts and use the Liturgy and personal forms of prayer to respond to the Spirit's call. God will never fail us, and we shall never fail God if we live in prayer by exercising the indwelling presence through habits of prayer. The prayers and devotions contained in this book are deeply rooted in the Catholic tradition, inspired by the Holy Scriptures, and intensely appealing to a vast spread of believers.

If we make these forms of devotion our own by consistent and faithful use, we will find ourselves formed and shaped by them in the image of Jesus. But we have to say our prayers slowly and carefully, with great respect, standing in awe of the God who is ever-present, all-powerful, and completely loving.

Novenas and triduums express our total dependence on God, the friend of the human race, the giver of all good gifts, the Old One who exists from all eternity, who upholds the entire universe from second to second, who stands outside all our finite categories, and whose name is simply Love.

Praying in a Group

Since triduums and novenas are often observed in a family or other group, directions are given in the text to assist active devotion by a family, prayer group, or parish. Novenas in the home are best done before the home altar.

❖ Pauses for quiet prayer are indicated after each psalm and Scripture reading and for spontaneous prayers of intercession in the novena prayer or litany.

❖ All group responses to the Leader of Prayer are printed in small capitals and preceded by a *tilde* [~], for example, ~AMEN.

❖ A *Leader* may be assisted by a *Reader* for the Scripture passage.

❖ The most convenient way to recite the hymns, psalms, and canticles is to have the *Leader* alternate the stanzas with the group and unite for the final—often Trinitarian—stanza.

❖ It is highly desirable that the group pause in silent prayer before beginning the vocal prayers and then taper off in quiet prayer at their conclusion.

❖ We may conclude our novena or triduum with a sign of peace to express our unity in Christ and in our prayer together.

❖ Postures for prayer are also important: standing, sitting, kneeling. Suggestions: *stand* to begin the opening verses, the hymn, and the psalm; *kneel* for the silent prayer after the psalm and for the psalm prayer; *sit* for the reading and the silent meditation after it; *stand* again for the canticle; *kneel* for the litany, the novena prayer, and the blessing.

The above suggestions may also be found helpful for those praying a novena or triduum by themselves.

Spiritual freedom and time constraints are the key to using any of the novenas printed in this book. Some people will want to use only the hymn, the psalm, or the Scripture reading, and then the novena prayer itself. Some may want to use just the litany and the novena prayer.

It is also well to remember that no scrupulosity should appear in the holding of novenas or triduums. If a day is missed for some pressing reason or by sheer forgetfulness, we must remember that there is nothing magical about the numbers nine or three. There is biblical and liturgical precedent for these numbers but no numerical obligation whatsoever.

Novenas to the Father, the Son, and the Holy Spirit

A Novena to God, Our Creator and Sustainer

After the inner life of the Blessed Trinity itself, the most mysterious event is creation and the continuous sustaining of the billions of galaxies that compose it. Theologians tell us that God overflows, as it were, in creation because God is essential love that knows no bounds. Why there is anything at all rather than nothing at all is the greatest of the natural mysteries and humbles us before the creative majesty of God. Our praise and thanksgiving are our normal and natural expressions of our recognition of our God who made heaven and earth and all that is in them.

In the name of our majestic Creator:
Father, ✝ Son, and Holy Spirit.
~Amen.

Hymn

I sing the mighty power of God
That made the mountains rise;
That spread the flowing seas abroad
And built the lofty skies.
I sing the wisdom that ordained
The sun to rule the day;
The moon shines full at God's command,
And all the stars obey.

I sing the goodness of the Lord
That filled the earth with food;
God formed the creatures with a word
And then pronounced them good.
Lord, how your wonders are displayed,
Where'er I turn my eyes;
If I survey the ground I tread,
Or gaze upon the skies.

There's not a plant or flower below
But makes your glories known;
And clouds arise and tempests blow,
By order from your throne;
While all that borrows life from you
Is ever in your care,
And everywhere that we can be,
You, God, are present there.

Isaac Watts (1674–1748)

PSALM 93   GOD REIGNS IN BEAUTY AND MAJESTY
ANTIPHON O Lord, HOW VAST ARE YOUR WORKS!

The Lord reigns and is robed in majesty;
the Lord is robed and is girded with strength.

The Lord has established the world;
it shall never be moved.
Your throne has been established from of old;
you are from everlasting!

The floods have lifted up, O Lord,
the floods have lifted up their voice,
the floods lift up their roaring.

Mightier than the thunder of many waters,
mightier than the waves of the sea,
the Lord on high is mighty!

Your decrees are very sure;
holiness befits your house,
O Lord, for evermore.

ANTIPHON O LORD, HOW VAST ARE YOUR WORKS!

Psalm Prayer
Let us pray *(pause for quiet prayer)*:

Almighty and everlasting God,
Creator and Preserver of the universe,
clothed in majesty and glory,
wrapped in light as in a robe:
We fall down in adoration before you,
asking you to permit us to worship you
in the holiness that comes from you alone;
through our Lord Jesus Christ your Son
who lives and reigns with you and the Holy Spirit,

one God, for ever and ever.

~Amen.

A Hymn to
Reading   **God's Majesty**   **Sirach 18:1–7**

He who lives for ever created the whole universe;
    the Lord alone is just.

To none has he given power to proclaim his
    works;

and who can search out his mighty deeds?

Who can measure his majestic power?

And who can fully recount his mercies?

It is not possible to diminish or increase them,

nor is it possible to fathom the wonders of the
    Lord.

When human beings have finished, they are just
    beginning,

and when they stop, they are still perplexed.

Silence

Response

I believe in God the Father almighty,

~The Creator of heaven and earth.

Canticle of the Creator   **Isaiah 40:28–31**

Antiphon In the beginning God created the
    heavens and the earth.

The Lord is the everlasting God,
    the Creator of the ends of the earth.

He does not faint or grow weary;
  his understanding is unsearchable.

He gives power to the faint,
  and strengthens the powerless.
Even youths will faint and be weary,
  and the young will fall exhausted;

but those who wait for the LORD shall renew their
  strength,
  they shall mount up with wings like eagles,
they shall run and not be weary,
  they shall walk and not faint.

Glory to the Holy and Undivided Trinity:
now and always and for ever and ever. Amen.

ANTIPHON IN THE BEGINNING GOD CREATED THE
  HEAVENS AND THE EARTH.

NOVENA PRAYER

Creator and Sustainer of the universe,
you maintain the billions of galaxies
and the dark matter of interstellar space.
In your wisdom you created everything that
  exists,
and especially the human race,
to acknowledge your power and your majesty.
In your mercy may we, your humble creatures,
bow down in adoration before you,
repent of our forgetfulness of you,
and lay before you all our needs.

(Here we state our needs.)

Merciful and mighty God,
hear us and help us, we humbly pray,
through the merits of Jesus the Messiah,
the one and only Savior of the world,
who lives and reigns with you and the Holy Spirit,
one God, for ever and ever.
~AMEN.

May almighty God,
the Father, the Son, and the Holy Spirit,
✝ bless us and keep us, now and for ever.
~AMEN.

A Novena to the Holy Trinity

A Trinitarian orientation is an essential element in popular piety. . . . All pious exercises in honor of the Blessed Virgin Mary and of the Angels and Saints have the Father as their final end, from whom all things come and to whom all things return; the incarnate, dead and resurrected Son is the only Mediator (1 Timothy 2:5) apart from whom access to the Father is impossible (John 14:6); the Holy Spirit is the only source of grace and sanctification.[1]

Devotion to the Trinity grew out of private devotion based on the many Trinitarian formulas in the Liturgy—the lesser Doxology ("Glory to the Father and to the Son and to the Holy Spirit . . .") and the greater Doxology ("Glory to God in the highest . . .")—and spread through the Latin West during and after the ninth century. After the celebration proliferated for several centuries, Pope John XXII extended the feast of the Blessed Trinity to the whole Latin Church in 1334. It is celebrated on the first Sunday after Pentecost.

A private or public novena or triduum may, of course, be celebrated at any time of the year.

Blessed be God: Father, ✝ Son, and Holy Spirit,
~Now and always and for ever and ever.
Amen.

Hymn

Eternal Trinity of love,
in peace and majesty you reign;
all things come forth from you alone;
to you they must return.

Creation lives and breathes in you,
sustained by your almighty will;
grant us to know you, God of truth,
in whom the questing mind is stilled.

Our Father, in the name of Christ,
unceasingly the Spirit send;
be with us everlasting God:
fulfill your purpose to the end.

We praise you, Godhead, One in Three,
immortal Trinity of light,
unchanging through eternal days
you live unmoved, serene in might.[2]

ANTIPHON Let us adore the true God,
ONE IN THREE AND THREE IN ONE.

O come, let us sing to the Lord;
let us make a joyful noise to the rock of our
    salvation!
Let us come into God's presence with
    thanksgiving;
let us make a joyful noise with songs of praise.

For the Lord is a great God,
and a great Ruler above all gods,
in whose hands are the depths of the earth
and also the heights of the mountains.
The sea belongs to God who made it,
and the dry land, because God formed it.

O come, let us worship and bow down,
let us kneel before the Lord our Maker!
For the Lord is our God,
we are the people of God's pasture,
the sheep of God's hand.

ANTIPHON LET US ADORE THE TRUE GOD,
ONE IN THREE AND THREE IN ONE.

PSALM PRAYER

Let us pray *(pause for quiet prayer)*:

Blessed and immortal Trinity,
almighty Father, only begotten Son, and Holy Spirit,
our first beginning and our last end:

We praise, adore, and magnify you
in the eternal mystery of your Being
and ask you to conduct us into endless bliss
with all the host of angels and the legion of saints
who worship you, now and for ever.
~AMEN.

READING   **THE DIVINE TRINITY**

I bow my knees before the Father, from whom
every family in heaven and on earth takes
its name. I pray that, according to the riches
of his glory, he may grant that you may be
strengthened in your inner being with power
through his Spirit, and that Christ may dwell
in your hearts through faith, as you are being
rooted and grounded in love. I pray that you
may have the power to comprehend, with all the
saints, what is the breadth and length and height
and depth, and to know the love of Christ that
surpasses knowledge, so that you may be filled
with all the fullness of God.

SILENCE

RESPONSE
Holy is God, holy and strong, alleluia!
~HOLY AND LIVING FOR EVER, ALLELUIA!

Song of the Church[3]
We praise you, O God,
we acclaim you as Lord;

all creation worships you,
the Father everlasting.

To you all angels, all the powers of heaven,
the cherubim and seraphim, sing in endless
    praise:
    Holy, holy, holy Lord, God of power and might,
    heaven and earth are full of your glory.

The glorious company of apostles praise you.
The noble fellowship of prophets praise you.
The white-robed army of martyrs praise you.

Throughout the world the holy Church acclaims
    you:
    Father, of majesty unbounded,
    your true and only Son, worthy of all praise,
    the Holy Spirit, advocate and guide.

You, Christ, are the king of glory,
the eternal Son of the Father.
When you took our flesh to set us free
you humbly chose the Virgin's womb.

You overcame the sting of death
and opened the kingdom of heaven to all
    believers.
You are seated at God's right hand in glory.
We believe that you will come to be our judge.

Come then, Lord, and help your people,
bought with the price of your own blood,
and bring us with your saints
to glory everlasting.

LITANY OF THE HOLY TRINITY

Abba, merciful and compassionate Father:
~HEAR US AND HAVE MERCY.

Abba, Lord of the angelic messengers
and of all the heavenly powers:
~HEAR US AND HAVE MERCY.

Abba, who created the work of your hands
by your only Son:
~HEAR US AND HAVE MERCY.

Lord Jesus, image of the invisible God
and firstborn of all creation:
~HEAR US AND HAVE MERCY.

Lord Jesus, light of the angels
and Savior of the human race:
~HEAR US AND HAVE MERCY.

Lord Jesus, firstborn from the dead
and head of your body, the Church:
~HEAR US AND HAVE MERCY.

Holy Spirit, advocate and guide of the faithful:
~HEAR US AND HAVE MERCY.

Holy Spirit, comforter and consoler of those who
mourn:
~HEAR US AND HAVE MERCY.

Holy Spirit, giver of life and teacher of truth:
~HEAR US AND HAVE MERCY.

(Pause for special intentions.)

By the intercession of the great Mother of God,
 Mary most holy, and of all those who adore the
 Most Holy Trinity:
~HEAR US AND HAVE MERCY.

PRAYER

God, we praise you:
Father all-powerful, Christ Lord and Savior,
 Spirit of love.
You reveal yourself in the depths of our being,
drawing us to share in your life and your love.
One God, three Persons,
be near to the people formed in your image,
close to the world your love brings to life.
We ask this, Father, Son, and Holy Spirit,
One God, true and living, for ever and ever.
~AMEN.[4]

Doxology

To God the Father,
who loves us and made us accepted in the Beloved:
To God the Son,
who loved us and freed us from our sins by his
 own blood:
To God the Holy Spirit,
who sheds the love of God abroad in our hearts:
To the one true God,
be all love and glory for time and for eternity.
~AMEN.

Bishop Thomas Ken (1631–1711)

A Novena in Honor
of the Holy Cross

The cross of Jesus is the main symbol of the Christian religion. Though once the sign of agony and shame reserved for vicious criminals, through Jesus it became the sign of salvation, life, and resurrection for us all.

The cross is given to us in Baptism and in Confirmation, when our foreheads are sealed with chrism with the sign of the cross. Since the earliest years of the Church we hear of Christians signing themselves constantly as they go about their daily prayer and work. This invocation of the cross and the Holy Trinity is a reaffirmation of our baptismal promises and therefore a rededication to the Christian way of life. A novena or triduum to the cross is a calling upon the Father, in virtue of the cross of Jesus, to come to our assistance in our time of need.

In the name of the Father, ✝ and of the Son, and of the Holy Spirit.
~AMEN.

The Lord of glory was nailed to the cross
~FOR THE SALVATION OF THE WORLD.

HYMN
Alone, in depths of woe,
Upon that scornful tree
Hangs Christ, redeemer of the world,
In shame and agony.

His feet and hands outstretched
By hammered nails are torn;

In mocking, on his head is thrust
A crown of bitter thorn.

Come, kneel before the Lord:
He shed for us his blood;
He died the victim of pure love
To make us one with God.[5]

PSALM 116:1–9   GOD DELIVERS JESUS FROM DEATH

ANTIPHON O God, YOU HAVE DELIVERED MY LIFE
FROM DEATH.

I love the Lord who has heard
my voice and my supplications,
and has listened to me
whenever I called.

The snares of death encompassed me;
the pangs of Sheol laid hold of me;
I suffered distress and anguish.
Then I called on the name of the Lord:
"O Lord, I pray, save my life!"

Gracious is the Lord, and righteous;
our God is merciful.
The Lord preserves the simple;
when I was brought low,
the Lord saved me.

Return, O my soul, to your rest;
for the Lord has dealt bountifully with you.
For you have delivered my life from death,
my eyes from tears,
my feet from stumbling;

I walk before the Lord
in the land of the living.

ANTIPHON O God, YOU HAVE DELIVERED MY LIFE
FROM DEATH.

PSALM PRAYER

Let us pray *(pause for quiet prayer):*

God of compassion,
you were attentive to your dear Son
when he cried out to you on the cross.
Helpless as he was, you saved him
from the snares of death
and the deadly darkness of the tomb.
May we walk with Jesus in the land of the living,
where he lives and reigns with you and the Holy
    Spirit,
one God, for ever and ever.
~AMEN.

DEATH ON
READING   **THE CROSS**   **JOHN 12:31–36**

Jesus said to the crowd, "Now is the judgment
of this world; now the ruler of this world will be
driven out. And I, when I am lifted up from the
earth, will draw all people to myself." He said this
to indicate the kind of death he was to die. The
crowd answered him, "We have heard from the
Law that the Messiah remains for ever. How can
you say that the Son of Man must be lifted up?
Who is this Son of Man?" Jesus said to them, "The

light is with you for a little longer. Walk while you have the light, so that the darkness may not overtake you. If you walk in the darkness, you do not know where you are going. While you have the light, believe in the light, so that you may become children of light."

SILENCE

RESPONSE

In the cross is victory, alleluia!

~IN THE CROSS IS POWER, ALLELUIA!

CANTICLE OF THE CROSS   **PHILIPPIANS 2:5–11**

ANTIPHON The sign of the cross will appear in the heavens, WHEN THE LORD RETURNS IN GLORY, ALLELUIA!

Christ Jesus, who, though he was in the form of God,
     did not regard equality with God
     as something to be exploited,
but emptied himself,
     taking the form of a slave,
     being born in human likeness.

And being found in human form,
     he humbled himself
     and became obedient to the point of death—
     even death on a cross.

Therefore God also highly exalted him
     and gave him the name
     that is above every name,

so that at the name of Jesus
   every knee should bend,
   in heaven and on earth and under the earth,
and every tongue should confess
   that Jesus Christ is Lord,
   to the glory of God the Father.

ANTIPHON THE SIGN OF THE CROSS WILL APPEAR
   IN THE HEAVENS, WHEN THE LORD RETURNS
   IN GLORY, ALLELUIA!

LITANY OF THE CROSS

Lord Jesus, you embraced your bitter passion
   and your dreadful death on the cross for us:
~LORD, HAVE MERCY.

Lord Jesus, you were condemned to the cross by
   Pontius Pilate:
~LORD, HAVE MERCY.

Lord Jesus, you stumbled again and again
   beneath the weight of the cross:
~LORD, HAVE MERCY.

Lord Jesus, you were fastened with nails
   to the wood of the cross:
~LORD, HAVE MERCY.

Lord Jesus, as you hung on the cross
   you were taunted and mocked by priests and
   soldiers:
~LORD, HAVE MERCY.

Lord Jesus, you forgave your enemies from the
 cross:
~LORD, HAVE MERCY.

Lord Jesus, you promised Paradise to a repentant
 criminal:
~LORD, HAVE MERCY.

Lord Jesus, from the cross you confided
 your sorrowful mother to your beloved disciple:
~LORD, HAVE MERCY.

Lord Jesus, you called out in agony on the cross
 and died with a great cry:
~LORD, HAVE MERCY.

Lord Jesus, you were taken down from the cross
 and laid in your mother's arms:
~LORD, HAVE MERCY.

Lord Jesus, you conquered death by your death
 and brought life to those in the grave:
~LORD, HAVE MERCY.

NOVENA PRAYER
As we stand beneath the shadow of your cross,
Lord and Savior of the world,
we put our trust in your undying love for us
in all our needs.
(Here we state our needs.)
You hear the voice of our hearts
as we worship, petition, and thank you,
now and always and for ever and ever.
~AMEN.

May the glorious passion of our Lord Jesus Christ
✝ bring us to the joys of paradise.
~AMEN.

A Novena to the Five Wounds of Jesus

One of the most impressive scenes in the resurrection Gospels is when "doubting" Thomas put his fingers into the hands and side of Jesus and reassured himself that the Lord was really risen (John 20:28). Our ancestors in the faith found great devotion to the five wounds of our Savior as they cried out in prayer with Thomas the apostle, "My Lord and my God!" They saw in the Five Wounds the indelible signs of God's unfailing love for us in Christ. The stunning wounds of prominent stigmatics like St. Francis of Assisi (1181–1226) and St. Pio of Pietrelcina (1887–1968), who bore the same five wounds in their flesh, stir up our devotion to the Five Wounds and encourage us to call upon God in virtue of those wounds to assist us in all our needs, both spiritual and temporal.

In the name of the Father, ✝ and of the Son,
and of the Holy Spirit.
~AMEN.

Jesus bore our sins in his body on the cross;
~BY HIS WOUNDS WE HAVE BEEN HEALED.

HYMN

O love, how deep, how broad, how high,
How passing thought and fantasy,

That God, the Son of God should take
Our mortal form for mortals' sake.

For us to evil power betrayed,
Scourged, mocked, in purple robe arrayed,
He bore the shameful cross and death,
For us gave up his dying breath.

For us he rose from death again;
For us he went on high to reign;
For us he sent the Spirit here
To guide, to strengthen, and to cheer.

All glory to our Lord and God
For love so deep, so high, so broad:
The Trinity whom we adore
For ever and for evermore.[6]

PSALM 22:1–2, 6–8, 14–21 GRAIL · JESUS CRIES OUT TO HIS FATHER

ANTIPHON They tear holes in my hands and my
feet AND LAY ME IN THE DUST OF DEATH.

My God, my God, why have you forsaken me?
You are far from my plea and the cry of my
distress.
O my God, I call by day and you give no reply;
I call by night and I find no peace.

I am a worm and no man,
the butt of all, laughingstock of the people.
All who see me deride me.
They curl their lips, they toss their heads.

"He trusted in the Lord, let him save him,
and release him if this is his friend."

Like water I am poured out,
disjointed are all my bones.
My heart has become like wax,
it is melted within my breast.
Parched as burnt clay is my throat,
my tongue cleaves to my jaws.

Many dogs have surrounded me,
a band of the wicked beset me.
They tear holes in my hands and my feet
and lay me in the dust of death.

I can count every one of my bones.
These people stare at me and gloat;
they divide my clothing among them.
They cast lots for my robe.

O Lord, do not leave me alone,
my strength, make haste to help me!
Rescue my soul from the sword,
my life from the grip of these dogs.
Save me from the jaws of these lions,
my soul from the horns of these oxen.

ANTIPHON THEY TEAR HOLES IN MY HANDS AND
MY FEET AND LAY ME IN THE DUST OF DEATH.

PSALM PRAYER
Let us pray *(pause for quiet prayer)*:
Lord Jesus Crucified,

your five priceless wounds
are indelible marks of love made visible.
On the cross of pain,
you begged your Father for help
and he rescued you from death and the grave
and raised you into glory.
Come now to our assistance
in our hour of need
and be our precious Savior.
Blessed be the holy name of Jesus.
~AMEN.

JESUS LIFTED UP
ON THE CROSS

READING   **JOHN 3:14–17**

Jesus said, "Just as Moses lifted up the serpent
in the wilderness, so must the Son of Man be
lifted up, that whoever believes in him may have
eternal life. For God so loved the world that he
gave his only Son, so that everyone who believes
in him may not perish but may have eternal life.
Indeed, God did not send the Son into the world
to condemn the world, but in order that the world
might be saved through him."

SILENCE

RESPONSE

We adore you, O Christ, and we bless you,
~FOR BY YOUR HOLY CROSS YOU HAVE REDEEMED
   THE WORLD.

LITANY OF THE LIFE-GIVING PASSION

Jesus, our blessed Savior, you embraced
    the bitter passion for us and for our salvation:
~LORD, HAVE MERCY.

Friend of the human race, you accepted the cross
    and your five agonizing wounds for us:
~LORD, HAVE MERCY.

Man of Sorrows, the wicked tore holes in your
    hands and feet and laid you in the dust of
    death:
~LORD, HAVE MERCY.

Your beauty was marred to give us back the
    splendor of God:
~LORD, HAVE MERCY.

By your wounds you vanquished hell
    and put dark death to flight:
~LORD, HAVE MERCY.

By your piteous death on the cross
    we are delivered from death and decay:
~LORD, HAVE MERCY.

By the prayers of the Mother of Sorrows
    and of all the martyrs and saints:
~LORD, HAVE MERCY.

NOVENA PRAYER

Father of mercies,
as we venerate Jesus' five precious wounds,
you promise us everything we need.

May we share in all the blessings they bring us
and especially
(Here we state our needs.)
Be praised and thanked for your loving-kindness
to us and to all who worship the passion,
death, and resurrection of our blessed Savior,
who lives and reigns with you and the Holy Spirit,
now and for ever.
~Amen.

By his holy and glorious wounds
may Christ Jesus ✝ protect us and keep us.
~Amen.

A Novena to the
Sacred Heart of Jesus

From the time the risen Jesus encouraged doubting
Thomas to put his fingers into his wounds (John 20:27),
Christians have been devoted to the Five Wounds and
especially to the wound in his sacred heart that poured
out blood and water for our salvation (John 19:34).
Saints and mystics down through the ages have found
in the heart of Jesus the supreme symbol of his love
for us, both collectively and individually. St. Augustine
of Hippo helps us to consider what is at stake in this
wound of Christ:

*Access is possible: Christ is the door. It was
opened for you when his side was opened by
the lance. Remember what flowed out from his
side: choose where you want to enter Christ.
From the side of Christ as he hung dying on the
Cross there flowed out blood and water, when*

it was pierced by a lance. Your purification is in that water, your redemption is in that blood.[7]

Thanks to a bevy of seventeenth-century saints who venerated the heart of Jesus—Margaret Mary Alacoque (1647–1690), John Eudes (1601–1680), and Claude de la Colombiére, SJ (1641–1682)—the Church produced fresh devotion to the Sacred Heart in the form of the Nine Fridays, the Holy Hour, and a special feast in honor of the Sacred Heart of Jesus. In the United States the solemnity of the Sacred Heart is celebrated on the Friday following the second Sunday after Pentecost. As a novena or triduum this devotion may be used at any time.

In the name of the Father, ✝ and of the Son, and of the Holy Spirit.
~AMEN.

When I see the blood, I will pass over you,
~AND NO PLAGUE SHALL DESTROY YOU.

The blood of Jesus shall be a sign for you
~ON THE HOUSES WHERE YOU LIVE.

HYMN

All you who seek a comfort sure
In trouble and distress,
Whatever sorrow burdens you,
Whatever griefs oppress:

When Jesus gave himself for us
And died upon the tree,
His heart was pierced for love of us;
He died to set us free.

A Novena to the Sacret Heart of Jesus **31**

Now hear him as he speaks to us
Those words for ever blest:
"All you who labor, come to me,
And I will give you rest."

O Heart adored by saints on high,
And hope of sinners here,
We place our every trust in you
And lift to you our prayer.[8]

PSALM 36:5–11   GOD'S GREAT GOODNESS[9]

ANTIPHON O God, HOW PRECIOUS IS YOUR
   CONSTANT LOVE!

LORD, your constant love reaches the heavens;
your faithfulness extends to the skies.
Your righteousness is towering like the
   mountains;
your justice is like the depths of the sea.
People and animals are in your care.

How precious, O God, is your constant love!
We find protection under the shadow of your
   wings.
We feast on the abundant food you provide;
you let us drink from the river of your goodness.
You are the source of all life,
and because of your light we see the light.

Continue to love those who know you
and do good to those who are righteous.
Do not let proud people attack me
or the wicked make me run away.

ANTIPHON O GOD, HOW PRECIOUS IS YOUR
   CONSTANT LOVE!

PSALM PRAYER

Let us pray *(pause for quiet prayer)*:

Sacred Heart of Jesus,
how precious is your love for us.
Keep on loving those who know you
and hide us in the shadow of your cross
as we seek your mercy and your help
in time of need.
You live and reign, now and for ever.
~AMEN.

	THE GOSPEL	**JOHN**
READING	**IN BRIEF**	**3:16, 35–36**

God so loved the world that he gave his only Son,
so that everyone who believes in him may not
perish but may have eternal life. The Father loves
the Son and has placed all things in his hands.
Whoever believes in the Son has eternal life;
whoever disobeys the Son will not see life, but
must endure God's wrath.

SILENCE

RESPONSE

Take my yoke upon you and learn from me,
   alleluia!
~FOR I AM MEEK AND HUMBLE OF HEART,
   ALLELUIA!

Canticle of Isaiah the Prophet 12:2–6[10]

Antiphon The plans of God's heart stand from age to age.

Behold God is my salvation;
I will trust and will not be afraid,
for the Lord God is my strength and my song;
and has become my salvation.

With joy you will draw water from the wells of
    salvation,
and in that day all of you will say:
Give thanks and call upon the name of the Lord,
make known among the nations
what the Lord has done,
proclaim that the name of the Lord is exalted.

Sing praises, for the Lord has triumphed
    gloriously;
let this be known in all the earth.
Shout and sing for joy, you people of God,
for great in your midst is the Holy One.

Glory to the Holy and Undivided Trinity:
now and always and for ever and ever. Amen.

Antiphon The plans of God's heart stand
from age to age.

Litany of the Sacred Heart of Jesus (see pages 246–248)

NOVENA PRAYER

Jesus, Savior of the world,

in your Holy Gospel you tell us:

"Ask, and it will be given you; search, and you will
find; knock, and the door will be opened for
you" (Matthew 7:7).

Moved by your divine promises,

I come before you to ask

(Here we state our needs.)

I address you as my Savior,

whose heart is an inexhaustible source of grace
and mercy.

Sacred Heart of Jesus,

friend of the human race,

consoler of the afflicted,

strength of those overwhelmed by their trials,

light of those who walk in darkness

or in the shadow of death,

I put my whole trust in you.

Blessed be Jesus Christ, true God and true man.

~AMEN.

Sacred Heart of Jesus, have † mercy on me and
mine.

~AMEN.

A Novena to the
Precious Blood of Christ

The precious blood of Jesus—poured out for us at his circumcision, in his agony in the Garden of Gethsemane, at his flogging and crowning with thorns, on his bloodstained path to Golgotha, at his nailing to the cross, by his pierced side—is a vivid depiction and sign of God's undying love for us.

The renowned English mystic Blessed Julian of Norwich (c. 1342–1423) helps us contemplate Jesus crucified and the efficacy of his precious blood:

The precious blood of our Lord Jesus Christ, as truly as it is most precious, so truly is it most plentiful. Behold and see the power of this most precious plenty of his precious blood. It descended into hell and broke its bonds, and delivered all who were there and who belong to the court of heaven. The precious plenty of his precious blood overflows all the earth and is ready to wash from their sins all creatures who are, have been and will be of good will. The precious plenty of his precious blood ascended into heaven in the blessed body of our Lord Jesus Christ, and it is flowing there in him, praying to the Father for us, and this is and will be so long as we have need. And furthermore, it flows in all heaven, rejoicing in the salvation of all humankind which is and will be there, and filling up the number which is lacking.[11]

Blessed ✝ be the most precious blood of Jesus.
~BY HIS WOUNDS WE HAVE BEEN HEALED.

When I survey the wondrous Cross
Where the young Prince of Glory died,
My richest gain I count but loss,
And pour contempt on all my pride.

Forbid it, Lord, that I should boast
Save in the death of Christ, my God;
All the vain things that charm me most,
I sacrifice them to his blood.

See from his head, his hands, his feet,
Sorrow and love flow mingled down;
Did e'er such love and sorrow meet?
Or thorns compose so rich a crown?

His dying crimson like a robe
Spreads o'er his body on the Tree,
Then am I dead to all the globe,
And all the globe is dead to me.

Were the whole realm of nature mine,
That were a present far too small;
Love so amazing, so divine,
Demands my soul, my life, my all.

Isaac Watts (1674–1748)

ANTIPHON We are your people,
BOUGHT WITH THE PRICE OF YOUR OWN BLOOD.

Preserve me, O God, for in you I take refuge.
I say to the Lord, "O Lord, you are my fortune,
    only you!"

The Lord is my chosen portion and my cup;
you hold my lot.
The boundary lines have fallen for me in pleasant
    places;
I have a goodly heritage.

I bless the Lord who gives me counsel;
my heart also instructs me in the night.
I have set the Lord always before me;
the Lord is at my right hand;
I shall not be moved.

Therefore my heart is glad, and my soul rejoices;
my body also dwells secure.
For you do not give me up to Sheol,
or let your godly one see the Pit.

You show me the path of life;
in your presence there is fullness of joy,
in your right hand are pleasures for evermore.

ANTIPHON WE ARE YOUR PEOPLE,
BOUGHT WITH THE PRICE OF YOUR OWN BLOOD.

PSALM PRAYER
Let us pray *(pause for quiet prayer):*

Abba, dear Father,
by Christ's precious blood
the world is redeemed
and we are reconciled to you.
By the power of that same precious blood
defend us against all the evils of this life,
making peace by the blood of his cross.
We ask this through the same Christ our Lord.
~AMEN.

READING

JESUS, OUR HIGH PRIEST   **1 PETER 1:18–20**

You know that you were ransomed from the futile ways inherited from your ancestors, not with perishable things like silver or gold, but with the precious blood of Christ, like that of a lamb without defect or blemish. He was destined before the foundation of the world, but was revealed at the end of the ages for your sake.

SILENCE

RESPONSE

You have redeemed us with your blood, O Lord,
~AND HAVE MADE US A KINGDOM FOR OUR GOD.

CANTICLE OF THE LAMB OF GOD   **REVELATION 4:11; 5:9–10, 12**

ANTIPHON Help your people, Lord,
BOUGHT WITH THE PRICE OF YOUR OWN BLOOD.

You are worthy, our Lord and God,
to receive glory and honor and power,

for you created all things,
and by your will they existed and were created.

You are worthy, O Christ,
to take the scroll and to open its seals,
for you were slaughtered
and by your blood you ransomed for God
saints from every tribe and language and people
and nation;
you have made them to be a kingdom and priests
serving our God, and they will reign on earth.

Worthy is the Lamb that was slaughtered
to receive power and wealth and wisdom and
might
and honor and glory and blessing.

ANTIPHON HELP YOUR PEOPLE, LORD,
BOUGHT WITH THE PRICE OF YOUR OWN BLOOD.

LITANY OF THE PRECIOUS BLOOD OF JESUS
(SEE PAGES 248–251)

NOVENA PRAYER
Lord Jesus, friend of the human race,
you shed your blood for us seven times
during your life on earth.
As we offer the chalice of blessing
without ceasing on our altars,
forgive us our sins,
and remember us in all our needs,
especially

(Here we state our needs.)

In virtue of your precious blood,
save us from the time of trial
and deliver us from the evil one.
You live and reign with the Father and the Holy
    Spirit,
 one God, for ever and ever.
~Amen.

May the precious plenty of Christ's precious blood
† wash us from all sin.
~Amen.

A Novena in Honor
of the Blessed Sacrament

Since a portion of the Holy Eucharist is reserved after
Mass for the sake of the sick and dying, over the centuries believers have become more and more aware
of the sacramental presence of the Lord Jesus in our
churches. Several private and public forms of devotion
have come to satisfy and encourage such awareness:
visits of prayer before the reserved Sacrament in the
tabernacle; benediction of the Blessed Sacrament;
holy hours of prayer before the tabernacle or before the
Host exposed in a monstrance; the Forty Hours devotion; processions with the Blessed Sacrament on the
feast of Corpus Christi or on other occasions.

This devotion may also be used on the eve of a First
Communion or its anniversary, or as a preparation for
Viaticum.

In the name † of the Father, and of the Son,
and of the Holy Spirit.
~Amen.

As often as you eat this bread and drink the cup,
~You proclaim the Lord's death until he
comes.

Hymn to the Blessed Sacrament

Hail our Savior's glorious Body,
Which his Virgin Mother bore;
Hail the Blood, which shed for sinners,
Did a broken world restore;
Hail the sacrament most holy,
Flesh and Blood of Christ adore!

To the Virgin, for our healing,
His own Son the Father sends;
From the Father's love proceeding
Sower, seed, and Word descends;
Wondrous life of Word incarnate
With his greatest wonder ends!

On that paschal evening see him
With the chosen twelve recline,
To the old law still obedient
In its feast of love divine;
Love divine the new law giving,
Gives himself as Bread and Wine!

By his word the Word almighty
Makes of bread his flesh indeed;

Wine becomes his very lifeblood:
Faith God's living Word must heed!
Faith alone may safely guide us
Where the senses cannot lead!

Come, adore this wondrous presence;
Bow to Christ, the source of grace!
Here is kept the ancient promise
Of God's earthly dwelling place!
Sight is blind before God's glory,
Faith alone may see his face!

Glory be to God the Father,
Praise to his coequal Son,
Adoration to the Spirit,
Bond of love, in Godhead one!
Blest be God by all creation
Joyously while ages run![12]

PSALM 116:12–19   A PSALM OF THANKSGIVING

ANTIPHON I will offer to you THE SACRIFICE OF
THANKSGIVING, ALLELUIA!

What shall I return to the Lord
for all God's gifts to me?
I will lift up the cup of salvation
and call on the name of the Lord,

I will pay my vows to the Lord
in the presence of all God's people.

Precious in the sight of the Lord
is the death of the faithful.
O Lord, I am your servant;

I am your servant, the child of your handmaid.
You have loosed my bonds.

I will offer to you the sacrifice of thanksgiving
and call on the name of the Lord.
I will pay my vows to the Lord,
in the presence of all God's people,
in the courts of the house of the Lord,
in your midst, O Jerusalem.

ANTIPHON I WILL OFFER TO YOU THE SACRIFICE
OF THANKSGIVING, ALLELUIA!

PSALM PRAYER
Let us pray *(pause for quiet prayer):*

Lord Jesus Christ,
we worship you living among us
in the sacrament of your body and blood.
May we offer to your Father in heaven
the broken bread of undivided love.
May we offer to our brothers and sisters
a life poured out in loving service of that kingdom
where you live with the Father and the Holy Spirit,
one God, for ever and ever.
~AMEN.[13]

READING   THE DAILY SACRIFICE   MALACHI 1:11
From the rising of the sun to its setting my
name is great among the nations, and in every
place incense is offered to my name, and a pure
offering; for my name is great among the nations,
says the LORD of hosts.

RESPONSE

I am the living bread that came down from
heaven, alleluia!

~WHOEVER EATS OF THIS BREAD WILL LIVE FOR
EVER, ALLELUIA!

CANTICLE OF WISDOM (16:20–21, 26)

ANTIPHON Whoever comes to me WILL NEVER BE
HUNGRY, AND WHOEVER BELIEVES IN ME WILL
NEVER BE THIRSTY, ALLELUIA!

You gave your people food of angels
and without their toil
you supplied them from heaven
with bread ready to eat,
providing every pleasure
and suited to every taste.

For your sustenance manifested
your sweetness toward your children;
and the bread, ministering to the desire
of everyone who took it,
was changed to suit everyone's liking,

so that your children,
whom you loved, O Lord, might learn
that it is not the production of crops
that feeds humankind
but that your word sustains
those who trust in you.

Glory to the Holy and Undivided Trinity:
now and always and for ever and ever. Amen.

ANTIPHON WHOEVER COMES TO ME WILL NEVER
BE HUNGRY, AND WHOEVER BELIEVES IN ME
WILL NEVER BE THIRSTY, ALLELUIA!

LITANY OF THE BLESSED SACRAMENT OF THE ALTAR (SEE PAGES 251–253)

(SEE PAGES 251–253)

NOVENA PRAYER

Lord Jesus Christ,
as we who worship you
in the Blessed Sacrament of the Altar,
may we discover your help in time of need.
(Here we state our needs.)
Just as your presence is everlasting
may your help sustain us in every necessity;
you live and reign with the Father and the Holy
    Spirit,
one God, for ever and ever.
~AMEN.

May the heart of Jesus
in the most Blessed Sacrament
be praised, adored, and loved,
with grateful affection,
at every moment,
in all the tabernacles of the world,
even unto the end of time.
~AMEN.

A Novena to the Infant of Prague

One of the favorite devotions of St. Teresa of Ávila (1515–1582) was to Christ, the Child of Bethlehem and Nazareth. It honors the Word of God as a human child dependent on his earthly parents in the silence of his hidden life. Another Carmelite, St. Thérèse of the Child Jesus (1873–1897), built her whole spiritual life around the simplicity and littleness of the Christ Child. Whenever we make use of this novena, we immerse ourselves in the profound humility of the Godhead buried in the Word Incarnate for us and our salvation. The "Infant of Prague" is a miracle-working statue of the Christ Child enshrined in the hearts and homes of the Carmelite Order.

Blessed ✝ be the Child of Bethlehem and
   Nazareth,

~WHO BECAME HUMAN THAT WE MIGHT BECOME
   DIVINE!

HYMN

Love came down at Christmas,
Love all lovely, Love divine;
Love was born at Christmas,
Star and angels gave the sign.

Worship we the Godhead,
Love incarnate, Love divine;
Worship we our Jesus:
But wherewith for sacred sign?

Love shall be our token,
Love be yours and love be mine,

Love to God and all men,
Love for plea and gift and sign.[14]

PSALM 67 PRAISE THE MESSIAH, MARY'S SON

ANTIPHON Let the peoples praise you, O God;
LET ALL THE PEOPLES PRAISE YOU!

O God, be gracious to us and bless us
and make your face to shine upon us,
that your way may be known upon earth,
your saving power among all nations.

Let the peoples praise you, O God,
let all the peoples praise you!

Let the nations be glad and sing for joy,
for you judge the peoples with equity
and guide the nations of the earth.

Let the peoples praise you, O God,
let all the peoples praise you!

The earth has yielded its increase;
God, our God, has blessed us.
May God still give us blessing;
let all the ends of the earth fear God!

ANTIPHON LET THE PEOPLES PRAISE YOU, O GOD,
LET ALL THE PEOPLES PRAISE YOU!

PSALM PRAYER

Let us pray *(pause for quiet prayer):*
Heavenly Father,
may the light of Christ's face shine upon us
to illumine our minds and hearts

to love and serve you all the days of our life.
You preserve us at every moment
and rain down your blessings upon us.
Hear us and help us in all our needs
and enable us to praise you
till the ends of the earth stand in awe.
We ask this through Christ our Lord.
~Amen.

A Child

Reading   **Born for Us**   **Isaiah 9:2, 6**

The people who walked in darkness have seen a great light; those who lived in a land of deep darkness—on them light has shined. For a child has been born for us, a son given to us; authority rests upon his shoulders; and he is named Wonderful Counselor, Mighty God, Everlasting Father, Prince of Peace.

Silence

Response

He shall be called Emmanuel, alleluia!
~God-with-us, alleluia!

The Canticle of the Angels
(Gloria in excelsis Deo)[15]

Glory to God in the highest,
    and peace to God's people on earth.

Lord God, heavenly King,
almighty God and Father,
    we worship you, we give you thanks,
    we praise you for your glory.

Lord Jesus Christ, only Son of the Father,
Lord God, Lamb of God,
you take away the sin of the world:
    have mercy on us;
you are seated at the right hand of the Father:
    receive our prayer.

For you alone are the Holy One,
you alone are the Lord,
you alone are the Most High,
    Jesus Christ,
with the Holy Spirit,
in the glory of God the Father. Amen.

LITANY TO THE DIVINE CHILD

Lord Jesus, by your timeless generation of the
    Father:
~HEAR US AND HELP US, WE HUMBLY PRAY.

By your wondrous conception in time
    of the Blessed Virgin Mary:
~HEAR US AND HELP US, WE HUMBLY PRAY.

By your humble birth in the cave of Bethlehem:
~HEAR US AND HELP US, WE HUMBLY PRAY.

By your precious name, Jesus, given by angels
    to Mary and Joseph:
~HEAR US AND HELP US, WE HUMBLY PRAY.

By your splendid manifestation to the shepherds
    of Bethlehem and the wise men from the East:
~HEAR US AND HELP US, WE HUMBLY PRAY.

By your presentation in the Temple of Jerusalem
and your meeting with old Simeon and Anna:

~Hᴇᴀʀ ᴜs ᴀɴᴅ ʜᴇʟᴘ ᴜs, ᴡᴇ ʜᴜᴍʙʟʏ ᴘʀᴀʏ.

By your finding in the Temple after you were lost
for three days:

~Hᴇᴀʀ ᴜs ᴀɴᴅ ʜᴇʟᴘ ᴜs, ᴡᴇ ʜᴜᴍʙʟʏ ᴘʀᴀʏ.

By your docile obedience to Mary and Joseph
in the humble home of Nazareth:

~Hᴇᴀʀ ᴜs ᴀɴᴅ ʜᴇʟᴘ ᴜs, ᴡᴇ ʜᴜᴍʙʟʏ ᴘʀᴀʏ.

By the intercession of the great Mother of God,
Mary most holy, of St. Joseph her husband,
and of the whole company of heaven:

~Hᴇᴀʀ ᴜs ᴀɴᴅ ʜᴇʟᴘ ᴜs, ᴡᴇ ʜᴜᴍʙʟʏ ᴘʀᴀʏ.

Nᴏᴠᴇɴᴀ Pʀᴀʏᴇʀ

Word made flesh for our salvation,
incarnate by the Father's will
and the consent of the Virgin Mary:
Be pleased to hear our prayers
as we adore you seated on Mary's lap.
(Here we state our needs.)
You promised to hear all those
who pray to the Father in your name.
Hear us and help us now as you live and reign
with the Father and the Holy and life-giving
Spirit,
one God, for ever and ever.

~Aᴍᴇɴ.

May the Christ, the Child of Bethlehem and
Nazareth, † bless us and keep us.
~Amen.

A Novena to the Good Shepherd

One of the most expressive Gospel titles of Jesus is
that of the Good Shepherd (John 10:11–15), who loves
his sheep and is willing to die for them, actively protect-
ing them from the wolves who prowl about "looking for
someone to devour" (1 Peter 5:8). In all humility we are
called upon to become obedient members of his flock
and to seek and accept the fact that he desires to feed
and protect us. Clement of Rome reminds us of Christ's
humility in his epistle to the Corinthians:

> It is to the humble-minded that Christ belongs,
> not to those who exalt themselves above his
> flock. The Sceptre of the Divine Majesty, the
> Lord Jesus Christ, did not, for all his power,
> come clothed in boastful pomp and overween-
> ing pride, but in a humble frame of mind, as the
> Holy Spirit has told concerning him.[16]

Blessed be † the Good Shepherd.
~Who lays down his life for the sheep.

Hymn

Christ be with me, Christ within me,
Christ behind me, Christ before me,
Christ beside me, Christ to win me,
Christ to comfort and restore me.

Christ beneath me, Christ above me,
Christ in quiet, Christ in danger,

Christ in hearts of all that love me,
Christ in mouth of friend and stranger.[17]

PSALM 23   SHEPHERD AND HOST[18]

ANTIPHON When the chief shepherd appears,
YOU WILL RECEIVE THE GLORIOUS CROWN.

LORD, you are my shepherd;
nothing I shall want.
Fresh and green are the pastures
where you give me repose.
Near restful waters you lead me
to revive my drooping spirit.

You guide me along the right path;
you are true to your name.
If I should walk in the valley of darkness
no evil would I fear.
You are there with your crook and your staff;
with these you give me comfort.

You have prepared a banquet for me
in the sight of my foes.
My head you have anointed with oil;
my cup is overflowing.

Surely goodness and kindness shall follow me
all the days of my life.
In the LORD's own house shall I dwell
for ever and ever.

ANTIPHON WHEN THE CHIEF SHEPHERD APPEARS,
YOU WILL RECEIVE THE GLORIOUS CROWN.

Psalm Prayer

Let us pray *(pause for quiet prayer)*:

Good Shepherd of the flock,
you tend and feed and protect your chosen people
and only ask us to put our trust in your loving
care.
As host you entertain us at your welcome table
and anoint us with your Holy Spirit.
Make us ever thankful for all your blessings,
O Savior of the world,
living and reigning with the Father and the Holy
Spirit,
now and for ever.
~Amen.

Reading   Good Shepherd   John 10:11–15[19]

I am the good shepherd, who is willing to die
for the sheep. When the hired man, who is not
a shepherd and does not own the sheep, sees a
wolf coming, he leaves the sheep and runs away;
so the wolf snatches the sheep and scatters them.
The hired man runs away because he is only a
hired man and does not care about the sheep. I
am the good shepherd. As the Father knows me
and I know the Father, in the same way I know my
sheep and they know me. And I am willing to die
for them.

Silence

RESPONSE

No one takes my life away from me.

~I GIVE IT UP OUT OF MY OWN FREE WILL.

LITANY OF THE GOOD SHEPHERD

Most High God, Shepherd of Israel:

~HEAR US AND HELP US, WE HUMBLY PRAY.

Good Shepherd, who was willing to die for the sheep:

~HEAR US AND HELP US, WE HUMBLY PRAY.

Good Shepherd, who knows the name of each one of his sheep:

~HEAR US AND HELP US, WE HUMBLY PRAY.

Good Shepherd, who revives our drooping spirits:

~HEAR US AND HELP US, WE HUMBLY PRAY.

Good Shepherd, who goes after each sheep that strays:

~HEAR US AND HELP US, WE HUMBLY PRAY.

Good Shepherd, who rescues his sheep from the wolves:

~HEAR US AND HELP US, WE HUMBLY PRAY.

Good Shepherd, who guards and guides his wandering sheep:

~HEAR US AND HELP US, WE HUMBLY PRAY.

Good Shepherd, who hears the prayers of the whole flock:

~HEAR US AND HELP US, WE HUMBLY PRAY.

Good Shepherd, whose goodness and kindness
   follow us all the days of our life:
~HEAR US AND HELP US, WE HUMBLY PRAY.

Good Shepherd, who pastures his sheep through
   all eternity:
~HEAR US AND HELP US, WE HUMBLY PRAY.

NOVENA PRAYER
Jesus, Good Shepherd,
you tend your flock unceasingly
and know our every need.
May your crook and your staff always protect us
and guide us through all the troubles of this life.
(Here we state our needs.)
Good Jesus, remember us in your infinite mercy,
set us among the blessed of your Father,
and save us in the time of trial,
O Savior of the world,
living and reigning with the Father and the Holy
   Spirit,
now and for ever.
~AMEN.

May the great Shepherd of the flock,
by the blood that sealed an eternal covenant,
✝ bless us and keep us.
~AMEN.

A Novena to the Holy Spirit

All novenas originate from the nine days between the ascension of our Lord and the coming of the Holy Spirit on Pentecost Sunday. Mary, the apostles, the brothers of Jesus, and many other disciples spent these nine days in prayer, awaiting the promised Spirit of fire and light (Acts 1:12–14). This novena may be used each year between the Ascension and Pentecost; for the vigil of a Baptism or Confirmation or their anniversaries; and at any time to invoke the assistance of the Holy Spirit.

In the name of God: Source of all being,
✝ Eternal Word, and Life-giving Spirit.
~AMEN.

A pure heart create for me, O God,
~PUT A STEADFAST SPIRIT WITHIN ME.

HYMN TO THE HOLY SPIRIT
Like the murmur of the dove's song,
like the challenge of her flight,
like the vigour of the wind's rush,
like the new flame's eager might:
    come, Holy Spirit, come.

To the members of Christ's Body,
to the branches of the Vine,
to the Church in faith assembled,
to her midst as gift and sign:
    come, Holy Spirit, come.

With the healing of division,
with the ceaseless voice of prayer,
with the power to love and witness,
with the peace beyond compare:
   come, Holy Spirit, come.[20]

PSALM 27:1–6   THE HOUSEHOLD OF FAITH

ANTIPHON I baptize you with water;
HE WILL BAPTIZE YOU WITH THE HOLY SPIRIT
   AND WITH FIRE.

The LORD is my light and my salvation;
whom shall I fear?
The LORD is the strength of my life;
of whom shall I be afraid?

When evildoers assail me,
to devour my flesh,
my adversaries and foes
shall stumble and fall.

Though a host encamp against me,
my heart shall not fear;
though war arise against me,
yet I will be confident.

One thing I asked of the LORD,
that will I seek after;
that I may dwell in the house of the LORD
all the days of my life,
to behold the beauty of the LORD,
and to inquire in the LORD's temple.

The LORD will hide me in a shelter
in the day of trouble;
will conceal me under the cover of a tent,
and will set me high upon a rock.

Now my head is lifted up
above my enemies round about me;
and I will offer sacrifices in the LORD's tent
with shouts of joy;
I will sing and make melody to the LORD.

ANTIPHON I BAPTIZE YOU WITH WATER;
HE WILL BAPTIZE YOU WITH THE HOLY SPIRIT
   AND WITH FIRE.

PSALM PRAYER

Let us pray *(pause for quiet prayer)*:

Heavenly King, Consoler, Spirit of truth,
present in all places and filling all things,
treasury of blessing and giver of life:
Come and dwell in us,
cleanse us from every stain of sin,
and save our souls,
O gracious Lord.
~AMEN.[21]

POURING FORTH
READING   **OF THE SPIRIT**   **ISAIAH 44:1–5**[22]

The Lord says, "I am the LORD who created
you; from the time you were born, I have
helped you. Do not be afraid; you are my
servant, my chosen people whom I love. I

will give water to the thirsty land and make
streams flow on the dry ground. I will pour
out my spirit on your children and my blessing
on your descendants. They will thrive like
well-watered grass, like willows by streams of
running water. One by one, people will say, 'I
am the LORD's.' Each one will mark the name
of the LORD on his arms and call himself one
of God's people."

OR THIS
READING **LIVING WATER** **JOHN 7:37–39**

On the last day of the festival [of booths], the
great day, while Jesus was standing there, he
cried out, "Let anyone who is thirsty come to
me, and let the one who believes in me drink.
As the scripture has said, 'Out of the believer's
heart shall flow rivers of living water.'" Now
he said this about the Spirit, which believers
in him were to receive; for as yet there was no
Spirit, because Jesus was not yet glorified.

SILENCE

RESPONSE

Come, Holy Spirit, fill the hearts of your faithful,
~AND KINDLE IN THEM THE FIRE OF YOUR LOVE.

LITANY

For a fresh outpouring of the Holy Spirit on all
here present, let us pray to the Lord.
~LORD, HEAR OUR PRAYER.

For the welfare of God's holy Church, let us pray
to the Lord.

~LORD, HEAR OUR PRAYER.

For the seven precious gifts of the Holy Spirit,
let us pray to the Lord.

~LORD, HEAR OUR PRAYER.

For the virtues of faith, hope, and love, let us pray
to the Lord.

~LORD, HEAR OUR PRAYER.

For new life, joy, and peace among us, let us pray
to the Lord.

~LORD, HEAR OUR PRAYER.

For the unity and reconciliation of families and
nations, let us pray to the Lord.

~LORD, HEAR OUR PRAYER.

For our beloved dead who have fallen asleep in
Christ
(Here we state the names of our deceased.)
let us pray to the Lord.

~LORD, HEAR OUR PRAYER.

For all our needs, temporal and spiritual
(Here we state our needs.)
let us pray to the Lord.

~LORD, HEAR OUR PRAYER.

For the prayers of the Virgin Mary and of all the
saints, let us pray to the Lord.

~LORD, HEAR OUR PRAYER.

PRAYER

Be present, be present,
Holy Spirit of comfort and consolation,
and inspire and guide us into all truth,
as Jesus promised.
Be present to us in wind and fire
as you were to your friends at Pentecost
and give fresh life to our gospel witness,
now and for ever.
~AMEN.

Doxology

Blessing and honor and thanksgiving and praise,
more than we can utter, more than we can
    conceive,
be yours, O holy and glorious Trinity,
Father, Son, and Holy Spirit,
by all angels, by all human beings, and by all
    creatures,
now and for ever.
~AMEN.

Novenas to Mary, the Mother of God

Theotokos (Mother of God) is the exact title for the mother of Jesus, the God-Man. It first appeared in Egypt in the late second century and became the watchword of orthodox Christians everywhere. Because of the theological triumph of the Council of Ephesus in 431, this essential title of *Theotokos* was confirmed for Mary and gave rise to a wave of devotions in her honor that has continued through the centuries. Heartfelt devotion to the Blessed Virgin Mary is the mark of all Orthodox and Catholic Christians. The various Marian novenas are a concrete expression of such confident devotion.

A Saturday Devotion in Honor of Mary

Since the ninth century, Saturday each week has been set aside in the Latin Church to honor the Mother of God. This weekly memorial "is a remembrance of the maternal example and discipleship of the Blessed Virgin Mary who, strengthened by faith and hope, on that great Saturday on which Our Lord lay in the tomb, was the only one of the disciples to hold vigil in expectation of the Lord's resurrection; it is a prelude and

63

introduction to the celebration of Sunday, the weekly memorial of the resurrection of Christ; it is a sign that the Virgin Mary is continuously present and operative in the life of the Church."[23]

This Marian devotion is suitable for a novena of nine Saturdays or a triduum of three Saturdays. It may also be used to honor Our Lady of Lourdes and Our Lady of Fatima.

In the name of the Father, ✝ and of the Son, and of the Holy Spirit.
~AMEN.

Hymn

O Queen of heaven, to you the angels sing,
The Maiden-Mother of their Lord and King;
O Woman raised above the stars, receive
The homage of your children, sinless Eve.

O full of grace, in grace your womb did bear
Emmanuel, King David's promised heir;
O Eastern Gate, whom God had made his own,
By you God's glory came to Zion's throne.

O Burning Bush, you gave the world its light
When Christ your Son was born on Christmas
      night;
O Mary Queen, who bore God's holy One,
For us, your children, pray to God your Son.
~AMEN.[24]

**A MARIAN
ANTHEM**

ANTIPHON A great portent appeared in heaven:
A WOMAN CLOTHED WITH THE SUN, WITH THE
MOON UNDER HER FEET,
AND ON HER HEAD A CROWN OF TWELVE STARS.
ALLELUIA!

Who is this coming forth like the rising dawn,
fair as the moon, bright as the sun,
terrible as an army set in battle array?

~THIS IS THE GREAT MOTHER OF GOD, MARY
MOST HOLY, WHO WAS CONCEIVED IN GRACE.

Who is this coming up from the desert
like a column of incense smoke,
breathing of myrrh and frankincense,
and of every fine perfume.

~THIS IS THE GREAT MOTHER OF GOD, MARY
MOST HOLY, WHO BORE CHRIST WHOM THE
WHOLE WORLD CANNOT CONTAIN.

Who is this who ascends God's holy mountain
and stands in his sanctuary
with clean hands and a pure heart?

~THIS IS THE GREAT MOTHER OF GOD, MARY
MOST HOLY, WHO SITS WITH CHRIST ON HIS
STARRY THRONE.

Who is this who washes her hands in innocence,
joins the procession about God's altar,
and proclaims all God's wonders?

~This is the great Mother of God, Mary
most holy, who alone, without peer,
pleased our Lord Jesus Christ.

Who is this exalted above the choirs of angels
and raised to the heavenly throne?

~This is the great Mother of God, Mary
most holy, who intercedes for us with
our Lord Jesus Christ.

Antiphon A great portent appeared in
heaven:
a woman clothed with the sun, with the
moon under her feet,
and on her head a crown of twelve stars.
Alleluia!

Prayer

Let us pray *(pause for quiet prayer):*

Great and glorious God,
you are wonderful in all your saints
and above all in the Mother of our Savior.
By the power of her prayers,
may we come to share in her holiness
and that of the whole company of heaven.
We ask this through Christ our Lord.
~Amen.

READING

I came forth from the mouth of the Most High, and covered the earth like a mist. I dwelt in the highest heavens, and my throne was in a pillar of cloud. Alone I compassed the vault of heaven and traversed the depths of the abyss. Over waves of the sea, over all the earth, and over every people and nation I have held sway. Among all these I sought a resting place; in whose territory should I abide? In the beloved city he gave me a resting place, and in Jerusalem was my domain. I took root in an honored people, in the portion of the Lord, his heritage.

SILENCE

RESPONSE

Blest is the womb that bore you, O Christ, alleluia!

~AND BLEST THE BREASTS THAT NURSED YOU,
   ALLELUIA!

CANTICLE OF THE
BLESSED VIRGIN MARY LUKE 1:46–55[25]

ANTIPHON Great Mother of God, Mary most holy,
YOU ARE MORE WORTHY OF HONOR THAN THE
   CHERUBIM,
AND FAR MORE GLORIOUS THAN THE SERAPHIM!

My soul † proclaims the greatness of the Lord,
my spirit rejoices in God my Savior,
for you, Lord, have looked with favor on your
   lowly servant.

A Saturday Devotion in Honor of Mary **67**

From this day all generations will call me blessed:
　　you, the Almighty, have done great things for me
　　and holy is your name.
　　You have mercy on those who fear you,
　　from generation to generation.

You have shown strength with your arm
and scattered the proud in their conceit,
casting down the mighty from their thrones
　　and lifting up the lowly.
You have filled the hungry with good things
and sent the rich away empty.

You have come to the aid of your servant Israel,
to remember the promise of mercy,
the promise made to our forebears,
to Abraham and his children for ever.

Glory to the Father, and to the Son,
and to the Holy Spirit:
as it was in the beginning, is now,
and will be for ever. Amen.

ANTIPHON GREAT MOTHER OF GOD, MARY MOST
　　HOLY,
YOU ARE MORE WORTHY OF HONOR THAN THE
　　CHERUBIM
AND FAR MORE GLORIOUS THAN THE SERAPHIM!

LITANY OF THE BLESSED VIRGIN MARY (AKATHIST)

Hail, Mary! Hail, the restoration of the fallen Adam;
Hail, the redemption of the tears of Eve.
~INTERCEDE FOR US WITH THE LORD.

Hail, Mary! Height, hard to climb, for human minds;
Hail, depth, hard to explore, even for the eyes
of angels.
~INTERCEDE FOR US WITH THE LORD.

Hail, Mary! Throne of wisdom;
Hail, security and hope for all who call upon you.
~INTERCEDE FOR US WITH THE LORD.

Hail, Mary! Heavenly ladder by which God came
down to earth;
Hail, bridge leading from earth to heaven.
~INTERCEDE FOR US WITH THE LORD.

Hail, Mary! Favor of God to mortals;
Hail, access of mortals to God.
~INTERCEDE FOR US WITH THE LORD.

Hail, Mary! Mother of the Lamb and of the Good
Shepherd;
Hail, fold for the sheep of his pasture.
~INTERCEDE FOR US WITH THE LORD.

Hail, Mary! Never silent voice of the apostles;
Hail, never conquered courage of champions.
~INTERCEDE FOR US WITH THE LORD.

Hail, Mary! Mother of the Star that never sets;
Hail, dawn of the mystic day.
~INTERCEDE FOR US WITH THE LORD.

Hail, Mary! Guide of the wisdom of the faithful;
   Hail, joy of all generations.
      ~Intercede for us with the Lord.

Hail, Mary! Mother of God's own Son;
   Hail, Mother of the Church.
      ~Intercede for us with the Lord.[26]

Novena Prayer

We turn to you for protection,
holy Mother of God.
Listen to our prayers
and help us in our needs.
(Here we state our needs.)
Save us from every danger,
glorious and blessed Virgin.[27]

Prayer

Heavenly Father,
joy came into the world
by the passion, death, and resurrection
of your beloved Son, Jesus Christ our Lord.
By the prayers of his blessed mother Mary,
make us true disciples of Christ
and bring us to the happiness of eternal life.
We ask this through Jesus, our holy Savior.
~Amen.

Holy God, holy mighty One, holy immortal One,
born of the Blessed Virgin Mary,
† bless us and keep us.
~Amen.

A Novena to the Blessed Virgin Mary

Popular devotion to the Blessed Virgin Mary is an important and universal ecclesial phenomenon. Its expressions are multifarious and its motivation very profound, deriving as it does from the people of God's faith in, and love of Christ, the Redeemer of humankind, and from an awareness of the salvific mission entrusted to Mary of Nazareth, because of which she is mother not only of our Lord Jesus Christ, but also of humankind in the order of grace.[28]

This novena may be used in preparation for any Marian feast.

In the name of the Father, ✝ and of the Son, and of the Holy Spirit.
~Amen.

Hymn

Mary the dawn, Christ the perfect Day.
Mary the gate, Christ the heavenly Way.

Mary the root, Christ the mystic Vine.
Mary the grape, Christ the sacred Wine.

Mary the wheat, Christ the living Bread.
Mary the rosebush, Christ the Rose bloodred.

Mary the font, Christ the cleansing Flood.
Mary the chalice, Christ the saving Blood.

Mary the temple, Christ the temple's Lord.
Mary the shrine, Christ the God adored.

Mary the beacon, Christ the haven's Rest.
Mary the mirror, Christ the Vision blest.

Mary the mother, Christ the mother's Son.
By all things blest while endless ages run.[29]

PSALM 46   GOD IS WITH US[30]

ANTIPHON You are a crown of beauty, O Mary,
IN THE HAND OF THE LORD.

God is our shelter and strength,
always ready to help in times of trouble.
So we will not be afraid, even if the earth is
    shaken
and mountains fall into the ocean depths;
even if the seas roar and rage,
and the hills are shaken by the violence.

There is a river that brings joy to the city of God,
to the sacred house of the Most High.
God is in that city, and it will never be destroyed;
at early dawn God will come to its aid.
Nations are terrified, kingdoms are shaken;
God thunders, and the earth dissolves.

The LORD Almighty is with us;
the God of Jacob is our refuge.

Come and see what the LORD has done.
See what amazing things God has done on earth.
He stops wars all over the world;
breaks bows, destroys spears,
and sets shields on fire.

"Stop fighting and know that I am God,

supreme among the nations,
supreme over the world."

The LORD Almighty is with us;
the God of Jacob is our refuge.

ANTIPHON YOU ARE A CROWN OF BEAUTY, O
MARY, IN THE HAND OF THE LORD.

PSALM PRAYER

Let us pray *(pause for quiet prayer):*

Great Mother of God
and mother of all the living,
as we honor you in your mysteries,
listen to our devout prayers
and stand by us in our every need.
We reverence you and worship your divine Son
who is the Savior of the world
and our living Lord, now and for ever.
~AMEN.

GOOD NEWS
READING   **FOR MARY**   **LUKE 1:35, 37–38**

The angel said to Mary, "The Holy Spirit will
come upon you, and the power of the Most High
will overshadow you; therefore the child to be
born will be holy; he will be called Son of God.
For nothing will be impossible with God." Then
Mary said, "Here am I, the servant of the Lord; let
it be with me according to your word."

SILENCE

RESPONSE

Blessed are you among women, O Mary,
~AND BLESSED IS THE FRUIT OF YOUR WOMB,
    JESUS.

CANTICLE OF THE VIRGIN MARY   LUKE 1:46–55[31]

ANTIPHON A great portent appeared in heaven:
A WOMAN CLOTHED WITH THE SUN, WITH THE
    MOON UNDER HER FEET,
AND ON HER HEAD A CROWN OF TWELVE STARS.

My soul ✝ proclaims the greatness of the Lord,
my spirit rejoices in God my Savior,
for you, Lord, have looked with favor on your
    lowly servant.

From this day all generations will call me blessed:
    you, the Almighty, have done great things for
    me and holy is your name.
    You have mercy on those who fear you,
    from generation to generation.

You have shown strength with your arm
and scattered the proud in their conceit,
casting down the mighty from their thrones
    and lifting up the lowly.
You have filled the hungry with good things
and sent the rich away empty.

You have come to the aid of your servant Israel,
to remember the promise of mercy,

the promise made to our forebears,
to Abraham and his children for ever.

Glory to the Father, and to the Son,
and to the Holy Spirit:
as it was in the beginning, is now,
and will be for ever. Amen.

ANTIPHON A GREAT PORTENT APPEARED IN
 HEAVEN:
A WOMAN CLOTHED WITH THE SUN, WITH THE
 MOON UNDER HER FEET,
AND ON HER HEAD A CROWN OF TWELVE STARS.

LITANY OF LORETO (SEE PAGES 253–255)

NOVENA PRAYER

Blessed Savior,
we come before you in worship
to pay our vows at your shrine,
the glorious Virgin's lap,
where you are enthroned for our adoration.
Here we pray for ourselves,
and for the whole world besides
(Here we state our needs.)
and especially for the poor and afflicted,
the desolate and deprived peoples of the earth.
Blessed are you, O Christ, now and for ever.
~AMEN.

May the Virgin Mother mild
✝ bless us with her holy Child.
~Amen.

A Novena to
Our Lady of Guadalupe

Mary appeared in the New World just ten years after the brutal Spanish conquest of Mexico. Her affectionate encounters in December 1531 with St. Juan Diego, a poor but faithful campesino, and her promises of protection and compassion proclaimed her the Mother of the Americas, the consolation of the afflicted, and the special protector of the poor and oppressed. Her miraculous image is preserved and venerated in her basilica in Mexico City. Her feast day falls on December 12, the last day of her three appearances to Juan Diego, and is celebrated throughout the Americas. Many people make a novena to prepare for this very significant North American feast.

Mary conversed with Juan Diego and unveiled her precious will:

Know and be certain in your heart that I am the Ever-Virgin Holy Mary, Mother of the God of Great Truth, Teotl, of the One through Whom We live, the Creator of Persons, the Owner of What Is Near and Together, of the Lord of Heaven and Earth. I very much want and ardently desire that my hermitage be erected in this place. In it I will show and give to all people all my love, my compassion, my help, and my protection, because I am your merciful mother and the mother of all the nations that live on this earth who would love me, who would speak with me, who would search for me, and who would place their confidence in me. There I would hear their laments and remedy and cure all their miseries, misfortunes and sorrows.[32]

In the name of the Father, ✝ and of the Son, and of the Holy Spirit.

~Amen.

Blessed be the great Mother of God, Mary most holy.

~Blessed be the name of Mary, Virgin and Mother.

Hymn

Mother of Christ, our hope, our patroness,
Star of the sea, our beacon in distress,
Guide to the shores of everlasting day
God's holy people on their pilgrim way.

Virgin, in you God made his dwelling place;
Mother of all the living, full of grace,
Blessed are you: God's word you did believe;
"Yes" on your lips undid the "No" of Eve.

Daughter of God, who bore his holy One,
Dearest of all to Christ, your loving Son,
Show us his face, O Mother, as on earth,
Loving us all, you gave our Savior birth.[33]

A Marian Anthem   Judith 13:18–20; 15:9[34]

Antiphon All generations will call me blessed.

The Most High God has blessed you
more than any woman on earth.
How worthy of praise is the Lord God
who created heaven and earth!
He guided you as you cut off the head
of our deadliest enemy.

~All generations will call me blessed.

Your trust in God will never be forgotten
by those who tell of God's power.
May God give you everlasting honor
for what you have done.

~All generations will call me blessed.

May God reward you with blessings,
because you remained faithful to him
and did not hesitate to risk your own life
to relieve the oppression of your people.

~All generations will call me blessed.

You are Jerusalem's crowning glory,
the heroine of Israel,
the pride and joy of our people.

~All generations will call me blessed.

Glory to the Holy and Undivided Trinity:
Now and always and for ever and ever. Amen.

~All generations will call me blessed.

Prayer
Let us pray *(pause for quiet prayer):*

Great Mother of God, Mary most holy,
you risked everything in becoming
the Virgin-Mother of the Messiah.
May we never forget your faith and trust
in the grace and power of God
and rely on your prayers for us,
now and for ever.
~Amen.

READING   MARY OF NAZARETH   LUKE 1:26–28, 31–32

The angel Gabriel was sent by God to a town in
Galilee called Nazareth, to a virgin engaged to
a man whose name was Joseph, of the house of
David. The virgin's name was Mary. And he came
to her and said, "Greetings, favored one! The Lord
is with you. You will conceive in your womb and
bear a son, and you will name him Jesus. He will be
great, and will be called the Son of the Most High."

SILENCE

RESPONSE

Blessed are you among women,

~AND BLESSED IS THE FRUIT OF YOUR WOMB,
JESUS.

CANTICLE OF THE BLESSED VIRGIN MARY   LUKE 1:46–55[35]

ANTIPHON Radiant Mother of God, cause of our
joy, AND COMFORTER OF THE AFFLICTED, COME
TO OUR ASSISTANCE, ALLELUIA!

My soul † proclaims the greatness of the Lord,
my spirit rejoices in God my Savior,
for you, Lord, have looked with favor on your
lowly servant.

From this day all generations will call me blessed:
you, the Almighty, have done great things for
me and holy is your name.
You have mercy on those who fear you,
from generation to generation.

You have shown strength with your arm
and scattered the proud in their conceit,
casting down the mighty from their thrones
and lifting up the lowly.
You have filled the hungry with good things
and sent the rich away empty.

You have come to the aid of your servant Israel,
to remember the promise of mercy,
the promise made to our forebears,
to Abraham and his children for ever.

Glory to the Father, and to the Son,
and to the Holy Spirit:
as it was in the beginning, is now,
and will be for ever. Amen.

ANTIPHON RADIANT MOTHER OF GOD, CAUSE OF
OUR JOY, AND COMFORTER OF THE AFFLICTED,
COME TO OUR ASSISTANCE, ALLELUIA!

LITANY OF LORETO (SEE PAGES 253–255)

NOVENA PRAYER

Remember, most loving Virgin Mary,
never was it heard
that anyone who turned to you for help
was left unaided.
Inspired by this confidence,
though burdened by my sins,
I run to you for protection
for you are my mother.
(Here we state our needs.)
Mother of the Word of God,
do not despise my words of pleading
but be merciful and hear my prayer.[36]

PRAYER

God of power and mercy,
you blessed the Americas at Tepeyac
with the presence of the Virgin Mary of
    Guadalupe.
May her prayers help all men and women
to accept each other as brothers and sisters.
Through your justice present in our hearts
may social justice and peace reign in the world.
Please grant this through Christ our Lord.
~AMEN.[37]

May the Virgin Mary of Guadalupe
✝ be the joy and consolation of her people.
~AMEN.

A Novena to
Our Mother of Sorrows

In the mid-thirteenth century seven prominent citizens of Florence left civic life and founded a religious association to venerate Jesus' mother under the title "Our Lady of Sorrows." By the time this association was officially approved by Pope Benedict XI in 1304, it had grown into the Order of Servites, devoted to honoring Mary's seven sorrows. Today, in several Canadian and American cities (Winnipeg and Chicago, for example) Servite churches maintain perpetual novenas to the Sorrowful Mother. These novenas have become a great consolation to thousands of the afflicted and depressed of our time. As Mother of the Church and of each baptized person in particular, she is one to whom we turn for protection, for help in time of need, and for consolation in time of trouble and distress. Her feast day falls on September 15, the day after the Triumph of the Cross.

In the name of the Father, ✝ and of the Son, and of the Holy Spirit.
~Amen.

Hymn

The new Eve stands before the Tree;
Her dying Son speaks words of love:
He gives his Mother as our Queen
On earth below, in heaven above.

The second Adam sleeps in death,
His side is pierced, his heart unsealed;
The grace-filled Church, his sinless Bride,
In blood and water is revealed.

We thank you, Father, for the Church,
Where Christ is King and Mary Queen,
Where through your Spirit you unfold
A world of glory yet unseen. Amen.[38]

PSALM 124   GOD'S PROTECTION

ANTIPHON Happy are you who weep now;
YOU WILL LAUGH!

If it had not been the LORD who was on our side—
let Israel now say—
if it had not been the LORD who was on our side,
when foes rose up against us
then they would have swallowed us up alive,
when their anger was kindled against us;

then the flood would have swept us away,
the torrent would have gone over us;
then the raging waters
would have gone over us.

Blessed be the Lord
who has not given us
as prey to their teeth!
We have escaped as a bird
from the snare of the fowlers;
the snare is broken
and we have escaped!

Our help is in the name of the LORD,
who made heaven and earth.

ANTIPHON HAPPY ARE YOU WHO WEEP NOW;
YOU WILL LAUGH!

PSALM PRAYER

Let us pray *(pause for quiet prayer)*:

Mother of Sorrows,
finest fruit of redemption
and perfect disciple of your divine Son,
help us share the loving compassion
you showed him during your agony
at the foot of the cross.
Blessed be the name of Mary, Virgin and Mother.
~AMEN.

READING   TEARS   LAMENTATIONS 1:2, 12

She weeps bitterly in the night, with tears on her cheeks; among all her lovers she has no one to comfort her; all her friends have dealt treacherously with her, they have become her enemies. Is it nothing to you, all you who pass by? Look and see if there is any sorrow like my sorrow, which was brought upon me, which the LORD inflicted on the day of his fierce anger.

SILENCE

RESPONSE

Let us stand by the cross with Mary the Mother of Jesus,
~WHOSE SOUL WAS PIERCED BY A SWORD OF SORROW.

CANTICLE OF THE
BLESSED VIRGIN MARY   LUKE 1:46–55[39]

ANTIPHON Is this the woman WHO WAS CALLED
THE PERFECTION OF BEAUTY, THE JOY OF ALL THE
EARTH?

My soul † proclaims the greatness of the Lord,
my spirit rejoices in God my Savior,
for you, Lord, have looked with favor on your
    lowly servant.

From this day all generations will call me blessed:
    you, the Almighty, have done great things for me
    and holy is your name.
    You have mercy on those who fear you,
    from generation to generation.

You have shown strength with your arm
and scattered the proud in their conceit,
casting down the mighty from their thrones
    and lifting up the lowly.
You have filled the hungry with good things
and sent the rich away empty.

You have come to the aid of your servant Israel,
to remember the promise of mercy,
the promise made to our forebears,
to Abraham and his children for ever.

Glory to the Father, and to the Son,
and to the Holy Spirit:
as it was in the beginning, is now,
and will be for ever. Amen.

ANTIPHON IS THIS THE WOMAN WHO WAS CALLED THE PERFECTION OF BEAUTY, THE JOY OF ALL THE EARTH?

LITANY OF THE SEVEN SWORDS

Holy Mary, Mother of the Man of Sorrows:

As we recall the prophecies of old Simeon and Anna in the Temple:
~PRAY FOR US.

As we recall your flight into Egypt and the years of exile there:
~PRAY FOR US.

As we recall your loss of the boy Jesus in the Temple for three long days:
~PRAY FOR US.

As we recall your tragic meeting with Jesus on the way to Golgotha:
~PRAY FOR US.

As we recall you standing at the foot of the Cross with the beloved disciple and Mary Magdalene:
~PRAY FOR US.

As we recall the descent of Jesus from the Cross into your loving arms:
~PRAY FOR US.

As we recall the burial of Jesus in the rock-hewn tomb of Joseph of Arimathea:
~PRAY FOR US.

Novena Prayer

Jesus, Man of Sorrows and acquainted with grief,
as you were suffering and dying on the cross
your sweet Mother's soul was pierced
by a sword of sorrow and compassion.
By her prayers and tears,
listen to our requests and help us in our needs,
especially
(Here we state our needs.)
Please grant that we who meditate on Mary's
　　sorrows
may enjoy the fruit of your suffering and death
and rise with you to everlasting life,
where you live and reign as our victorious Lord,
now and for ever.
~Amen.

May the glorious passion of our Lord Jesus Christ
✝ bring us to the joys of paradise.
~Amen.

A Novena to
Our Lady of Mount Carmel

In the twelfth century a group of hermits, modeling themselves on Elijah the prophet, gathered on Mount Carmel in Palestine. Eventually they adopted a severe rule of life, recorded around 1208 by St. Albert, the Latin Patriarch of Jerusalem. When the order spread to Europe in the thirteenth century, its members became preachers as well as contemplatives, adopting a way of life like that of the Franciscans and Dominicans. In the later Middle Ages both religious women and laypeople became associated with the Order of Carmel. The latter wore some part of the habit of the order (for example, the brown scapular) and practiced special devotion to Our Lady of Mount Carmel, often the daily Little Office of the Virgin and the Saturday fast in Mary's honor.

Although some of the promises made in the late Middle Ages regarding the brown scapular are now considered spurious, its connection to the Three Orders of Carmel is considered spiritually valuable by all those who revere such outstanding saints as Teresa of Ávila, John of the Cross, Thérèse of Lisieux, Elizabeth of the Holy Trinity, and Edith Stein.

Blessed ✝ be the great Mother of God, Mary most holy!

~Blessed be the Mother of Carmel, Virgin and Mother!

Hymn to Our Lady of Mount Carmel

Mary of Carmel, crowned with heaven's glory,
Look on us, Mother, as we sing your praises:
Be with us always, joy of saints and angels,
Joy of creation.

Here on Mount Carmel peace is all around us:
Here is the garden where your children gather,
Praising God's goodness, voices raised in
    gladness,
One with our Mother.

Come to God's mountain, all who serve Our Lady:
Sing to God's glory, young and old together,

All hearts outpouring Mary's song of worship,
Thanking her Maker.

Sing to the Father, who exalts his handmaid;
Sing to God's wisdom, Son who chose his Mother;
Sing to their Spirit, Love that overshadowed
Mary, chaste Virgin.[40]

PSALM 138   THE LORD CARES FOR THE LOWLY[41]

ANTIPHON Blessed are you, O Virgin Mary,
AND WORTHY OF ALL PRAISE!

I thank you, LORD, with all my heart;
I sing praise to you before the gods.
I face your holy Temple,
bow down, and praise your name
because of your constant love and faithfulness,
because you have shown that your name
and your commands are supreme.
You answered me when I called to you;
with your strength you strengthened me.

All the kings of the world will praise you, LORD,
because they have heard your promises.
They will sing about what you have done
and about your great glory.
Even though you are so high above,
you care for the lowly,
and the proud cannot hide from you.

When I am surrounded by troubles,
you keep me safe.
You oppose my angry enemies

and save me by your power.
You will do everything you have promised;
LORD, your love is eternal.
Complete the work that you have begun.

ANTIPHON BLESSED ARE YOU, O VIRGIN MARY,
AND WORTHY OF ALL PRAISE!

PSALM PRAYER

Let us pray *(pause for quiet prayer):*

Lady of Mount Carmel,
living garden rich in flowers and fruits,
be our intercessor with your divine Son
who hears our every prayer
because he is love incarnate.
Blessed be the name of Mary, Virgin and Mother!
~AMEN.

	LADY OF	SONG OF
READING	**CARMEL**	**SOLOMON 6:4, 10**

You are beautiful as Tirzah, my love, comely
as Jerusalem, terrible as an army with banners.
"Who is this that looks forth like the dawn, fair
as the moon, bright as the sun, terrible as an army
with banners?"

SILENCE

RESPONSE

O Mary, fairest among women,
~YOU ARE ALTOGETHER BEAUTIFUL.

CANTICLE OF THE
BLESSED VIRGIN MARY   LUKE 1:46–55[42]

ANTIPHON Hail, Mary, FULL OF GRACE. THE LORD
IS WITH YOU.

My soul ✝ proclaims the greatness of the Lord,
my spirit rejoices in God my Savior,
for you, Lord, have looked with favor on your
    lowly servant.

From this day all generations will call me blessed:
    you, the Almighty, have done great things for me
    and holy is your name.
    You have mercy on those who fear you,
    from generation to generation.

You have shown strength with your arm
and scattered the proud in their conceit,
casting down the mighty from their thrones
    and lifting up the lowly.
You have filled the hungry with good things
and sent the rich away empty.

You have come to the aid of your servant Israel,
to remember the promise of mercy,
the promise made to our forebears,
to Abraham and his children for ever.

Glory to the Father, and to the Son,
and to the Holy Spirit:
as it was in the beginning, is now,
and will be for ever. Amen.

LITANY OF LORETO (SEE PAGES 253–255)

NOVENA PRAYER
Mother of Carmel,
cause of our joy,
you are a garden fountain,
a well of living water,
a flowing stream from Lebanon.
Please hear our prayers in all our needs.
(Here we state our needs.)
Be our safeguard and protector
for Jesus made you our blessed Mother,
the comfort of the troubled
and the help of Christians,
now and for ever.
~AMEN.

May the Word made flesh, full of grace and truth,
✝ bless us and keep us.
~AMEN.

A Novena to
Our Lady of the Rosary

Because of its intrinsic worth as a form of vocal and
contemplative prayer, the rosary has been a favorite
devotion of Catholics for centuries. Though endorsed
by numerous popes, it was Pope John Paul II who
recommended the rosary in a particularly warm and

personal way in his apostolic letter *Rosarium Virginis Mariae* (October 16, 2002). Even Mary herself has expressed her approval of the devotion in her many appearances at Lourdes, Fatima, and elsewhere.

A novena in her honor is often composed of five decades of the rosary each day with a form of novena prayer.

In the name of the Father, ✝ and of the Son, and of the Holy Spirit.
~AMEN.

HYMN

Hail, our Queen and Mother blest!
Joy when all was sadness,
life and hope you brought to earth,
Mother of our gladness.

Children of the sinful Eve,
sinless Eve befriend us,
exiled in this vale of tears:
strength and comfort send us.

Pray for us, O Patroness,
be our consolation!
Lead us home to see your Son,
Jesus, our salvation!

Gracious are you, full of grace,
loving as none other;
joy of heaven and joy of earth,
Mary, God's own Mother![43]

PSALM 113   GOD LIFTS UP THE LOWLY

ANTIPHON Holy Mary, Virgin of virgins,
YOU ARE THE PRIDE AND JOY OF YOUR PEOPLE.

Praise, O servants of the Lord
praise the name of the Lord!
Blessed be the name of the Lord
from this time forth and for evermore!
From the rising of the sun to its setting
the name of the Lord is to be praised!

The Lord is high above all nations,
God's glory above the heavens!
Who is like the Lord our God,
who is seated on high,
who looks far down
upon the heavens and the earth?

God raises the poor from the dust,
and lifts the needy from the ash heap,
to make them sit with nobles,
with the nobles of God's people.
God gives the barren woman a home,
making her the joyous mother of children.

ANTIPHON HOLY MARY, VIRGIN OF VIRGINS,
YOU ARE THE PRIDE AND JOY OF YOUR PEOPLE.

PSALM PRAYER

Let us pray *(pause for quiet prayer)*:

Queen of the Holy Rosary,
by the mysteries of your Son's life and death,
help us to walk the straight and narrow path

to our Father's heavenly home,
where you live and reign with your divine Son,
now and for ever.

~AMEN.

READING

BORN OF A WOMAN   **GALATIANS 4:4–6**

When the fullness of time had come, God sent
his Son, born of a woman, born under the law, in
order to redeem those who were under the law, so
that we might receive adoption as children. And
because you are children, God has sent the Spirit
of his Son into our hearts, crying, "Abba! Father!"

SILENCE

RESPONSE

Hail, Mary, full of grace, the Lord is with you.

~BLESSED ARE YOU AMONG WOMEN.

CANTICLE OF THE BLESSED VIRGIN MARY   LUKE 1:46–55[44]

ANTIPHON Virgin Mother of God AND GLORIOUS
    QUEEN OF THE UNIVERSE, INTERCEDE FOR US
    WITH THE LORD OUR GOD.

My soul † proclaims the greatness of the Lord,
my spirit rejoices in God my Savior,
for you, Lord, have looked with favor on your
    lowly servant.

From this day all generations will call me blessed:
    you, the Almighty, have done great things for me
    and holy is your name.

You have mercy on those who fear you,
from generation to generation.

You have shown strength with your arm
and scattered the proud in their conceit,
casting down the mighty from their thrones
    and lifting up the lowly.
You have filled the hungry with good things
and sent the rich away empty.

You have come to the aid of your servant Israel,
to remember the promise of mercy,
the promise made to our forebears,
to Abraham and his children for ever.

Glory to the Father, and to the Son,
and to the Holy Spirit:
as it was in the beginning, is now,
and will be for ever. Amen.

ANTIPHON VIRGIN MOTHER OF GOD AND
    GLORIOUS QUEEN OF THE UNIVERSE,
    INTERCEDE FOR US WITH THE LORD OUR GOD.

LITANY OF LORETO (SEE PAGES 253–255)

NOVENA PRAYER
Great Mother of God,
we revere the sacred mysteries of your holy rosary
and promise to pray it with attention and devotion.
Help us incorporate each mystery into our life
as we pray to you for help.

(Here we state our needs.)

Mother of mercy, hear our petitions,
for you are our constant intercessor
before the throne of your divine Son,
our blessed Savior Jesus Christ,
who lives and reigns with the Father and the Holy
    Spirit,
now and for ever.
~Amen.

May the blessing of almighty God,
the Father, the Son, and the Holy Spirit,
✝ descend upon us and remain with us for ever.
~Amen.

A Novena to
Our Lady of Perpetual Help

This novena centers on the miracle-working icon of Our Lady of Perpetual Help that is enshrined in the Redemptorist church in Rome. Wherever the order has spread throughout the world, it preaches and teaches devotion to Mary under this title and encourages people to make novenas to her for cures and other favors, both spiritual and temporal. Like the novena to the Mother of Sorrows, this novena is maintained in several well-known downtown churches in North America.

In the name of the Father, ✝ and of the Son,
and of the Holy Spirit.
~Amen.

CELTIC POEM TO THE VIRGIN MARY

The Virgin was seen coming,
the young Christ at her breast,
angels bowing in submission before them,
and the King of the Universe saying it was fitting.

The Virgin of ringlets most excellent,
Jesus more surpassing white than snow,
melodious Seraphs singing their praise,
and the King of the Universe saying it was fitting.

Mary, Mother of miracles, help us,
help us with thy strength,
bless the food, bless the board,
bless the ear, the corn, the victuals.

The Virgin most excellent of face,
Jesus more surpassing white than snow,
She like the moon rising over the hills,
He like the sun on the peaks of the mountains.[45]

PSALM 122   MARY IS GOD'S HOUSE[46]

ANTIPHON   Blessed be the great Mother of God,
MARY MOST HOLY!

I was glad when they said to me,
"Let us go to the LORD's house."
And now we are here,
standing inside the gates of Jerusalem!

Jerusalem is a city restored
in beautiful order and harmony.
This is where the tribes come,

the tribes of Israel,
to give thanks to the LORD
according to his command.
Here the kings of Israel
sat to judge their people.

Pray for the peace of Jerusalem:
"May those who love you prosper.
May there be peace inside your walls
and safety in your palaces."

For the sake of my relatives and friends
I say to Jerusalem, "Peace be with you!"
For the sake of the house of the LORD our God
I pray for your prosperity.

ANTIPHON BLESSED BE THE GREAT MOTHER OF
GOD, MARY MOST HOLY!

PSALM PRAYER

Let us pray *(pause for quiet prayer):*
Merciful Mother of the Christ Child at your
breast,
you who pondered his mysteries in your heart,
be now the Mother of miracles for us
and come to our assistance
when we ask for your help.
Blessed be the Morning Star of the universe.
~AMEN.

READING

Wisdom praises herself, and tells of her glory in the midst of her people. "I came forth from the mouth of the Most High, and covered the earth like a mist. I dwelt in the highest heavens, and my throne was in a pillar of cloud. Alone I compassed the vault of heaven and traversed the depths of the abyss. Over waves of the sea, over all the earth, and over every people and nation I have held sway. Among all these I sought a resting place; in whose territory should I abide? Thus in the beloved city he gave me a resting place, and in Jerusalem was my domain. I took root in an honored people, in the portion of the Lord, his heritage.

SILENCE

RESPONSE

Blest is the womb that bore you, O Lord,
~AND THE BREASTS THAT NURSED YOU.

CANTICLE OF THE BLESSED VIRGIN MARY LUKE 1:46–55[47]

ANTIPHON Hail, Mary, FULL OF GRACE. THE LORD IS WITH YOU.

My soul † proclaims the greatness of the Lord,
my spirit rejoices in God my Savior,
for you, Lord, have looked with favor on your
  lowly servant.

From this day all generations will call me blessed:
you, the Almighty, have done great things for me
and holy is your name.
You have mercy on those who fear you,
from generation to generation.

You have shown strength with your arm
and scattered the proud in their conceit,
casting down the mighty from their thrones
and lifting up the lowly.
You have filled the hungry with good things
and sent the rich away empty.

You have come to the aid of your servant Israel,
to remember the promise of mercy,
the promise made to our forebears,
to Abraham and his children for ever.

Glory to the Father, and to the Son,
and to the Holy Spirit:
as it was in the beginning, is now,
and will be for ever. Amen.

ANTIPHON HAIL, MARY, FULL OF GRACE. THE
LORD IS WITH YOU.

LITANY OF LORETO (SEE PAGES 253–255)

NOVENA PRAYER
Mother of Perpetual Help,
we want to be your devoted children,
loving you in all your mysteries
and in your care for the Christian people.

As we invoke your assistance,
hear us and help us, we humbly pray.
(Here we state our needs.)
Compassionate Virgin,
help of Christians, health of the sick,
and refuge of sinners,
through your intercession,
free us from the sorrows of this life
and lead us with you into the life to come.
Blessed is the name of Mary, Virgin and Mother.
~Amen.

May Christ, the Son of God and the Son of Mary,
✝ bless us and keep us.
~Amen.

A Novena to the Immaculate Heart of Mary

Just as the whole mystery of Christ can be typified
by its font, the heart of Jesus, so too the memorial of
the heart of Mary can summarize Mary's participation
in her Son's saving role—from the incarnation itself,
through his death and resurrection, to the gift of the
Holy Spirit on Pentecost. The feast is celebrated on
the first day after the solemnity of the Sacred Heart of
Jesus and is a liturgical sign of the close connection
between Mother and Son.

Devotion to the Immaculate Heart of Mary is
closely tied to the observance of the Five First
Saturdays. "This pious practice should be seen as
an opportunity to live intensely the paschal mystery

celebrated in the Eucharist, as inspired by the life of the Blessed Virgin Mary." [48]

In the name of the Father, ✝ and of the Son, and of the Holy Spirit.

~Amen.

Hymn

O heart of Mary, pure and fair
And free from sin's domain,
In Adam's fall you had no share;
In you there is no stain.

The fairest rose, which grew in thorns,
Your heart so full of grace
With spotless purity adorns
Our sinful fallen race.

The heart of Christ, by God's decree,
Was formed beneath your heart,
We long to love him worthily:
In your love give us part.

His words you pondered in your heart
With contemplation pure;
O may the grace which they impart,
In our weak hearts endure. [49]

A Marian Anthem   **Judith 13:18–20; 15:9** [50]

Antiphon All generations WILL CALL ME BLESSED.

The Most High God has blessed you
more than any woman on earth.
How worthy of praise is the Lord God

who created heaven and earth!
He guided you as you cut off the head
of our deadliest enemy.

~All generations will call me blessed.

Your trust in God will never be forgotten
by those who tell of God's power.
May God give you everlasting honor
for what you have done.

~All generations will call me blessed.

May God reward you with blessings,
because you remained faithful to him
and did not hesitate to risk your own life
to relieve the oppression of your people.

~All generations will call me blessed.

You are Jerusalem's crowning glory,
the heroine of Israel,
the pride and joy of our people.

~All generations will call me blessed.

Glory to the Holy and Undivided Trinity:
Now and always and for ever and ever. Amen.

Antiphon ~All generations will call me
  blessed.

Prayer

Let us pray *(pause for quiet prayer):*

Almighty and everlasting God,
by the cooperation of the Holy Spirit
you prepared the body and soul of Mary

to be a fit dwelling for your Son.
May we who rejoice in her memory
be freed by her loving prayers
both from present ills and from eternal death;
we ask this through Jesus Christ our Lord.
~AMEN.

HERE IS
READING   **YOUR MOTHER**   **JOHN 19:25–27**

Standing near the cross of Jesus were his mother,
and his mother's sister, Mary the wife of Clopas, and
Mary Magdalene. When Jesus saw his mother
and the disciple whom he loved standing beside
her, he said to his mother, "Woman, here is your
son." Then he said to the disciple, "Here is your
mother." And from that hour the disciple took her
into his own home.

SILENCE

RESPONSE

His mother pondered all these things
~IN HER IMMACULATE HEART.

CANTICLE OF THE
BLESSED VIRGIN MARY   **LUKE 1:46–55**[51]

ANTIPHON The Ruler of heaven and earth
NURSED AT HIS MOTHER'S BREAST.

My soul ✝ proclaims the greatness of the Lord,
my spirit rejoices in God my Savior,
for you, Lord, have looked with favor on your
    lowly servant.

From this day all generations will call me blessed:
    you, the Almighty, have done great things for me
    and holy is your name.
    You have mercy on those who fear you,
    from generation to generation.

You have shown strength with your arm
and scattered the proud in their conceit,
casting down the mighty from their thrones
and lifting up the lowly.
You have filled the hungry with good things
and sent the rich away empty.

You have come to the aid of your servant Israel,
to remember the promise of mercy,
the promise made to our forebears,
to Abraham and his children for ever.

Glory to the Father, and to the Son,
and to the Holy Spirit:
as it was in the beginning, is now,
and will be for ever. Amen.

ANTIPHON THE RULER OF HEAVEN AND EARTH
NURSED AT HIS MOTHER'S BREAST.

LITANY OF LORETO (SEE PAGES 253–255)

NOVENA PRAYER
God of power and might,
in the heart of the Virgin Mary
you prepared a dwelling worthy of the Holy Spirit.

By her loving prayers,
hear us in our time of need
and rescue us from our problems and anxieties.
(Here we state our needs.)
May we, too, be shrines of God's presence
and true disciples of our blessed Savior.
We ask this through Christ our Lord.
~Amen.

May the Virgin Mary mild
✝ bless us with her holy Child.
~Amen.

A Novena to Mary, Queen of Heaven

After her blessed falling asleep in death (her dormition), Mary was taken up into heavenly glory and crowned Queen of Heaven *(Regina coeli)*. Joined with her Son, the King of Glory, she, too, became the firstfruits of our human nature and a joint intercessor with him for ever. In every need and at every moment we have recourse to her, confident that she is our mother in time and in eternity.

Blessed be ✝ the great Mother of God, Mary most holy.
~Blessed be her glorious assumption.

Hymn
O glorious Lady, throned in rest,
Amidst the starry host above,

Who gave sweet nurture from your breast
To God, with pure maternal love.

O gate, through which has passed the King,
O hall, whence Light shone through the gloom:
The ransomed nations praise and sing
Life given from the Virgin's womb.

O Lord, the Virgin-born, to you
Eternal praise and laud are due
Whom with the Father we adore
And Spirit blest for evermore.[52]

PSALM 117   PRAISE THE LORD!

ANTIPHON Mary is assumed INTO GLORY,
   ALLELUIA!

Praise the Lord, all nations!
Extol the Lord, all peoples!

~MARY IS ASSUMED INTO GLORY, ALLELUIA!

Great is the Lord's steadfast love for us!
The faithfulness of the Lord endures for ever!

~MARY IS ASSUMED INTO GLORY, ALLELUIA!

Glory to the Father, and to the Son,
and to the Holy Spirit:

~MARY IS ASSUMED INTO GLORY, ALLELUIA!

As it was in the beginning, is now,
and will be for ever. Amen.

~MARY IS ASSUMED INTO GLORY, ALLELUIA!

PSALM PRAYER

Let us pray *(pause for quiet prayer):*

Heavenly Father,
in your plan of salvation
the holy Mother of God
is our mother too.
When she fell asleep in death
she did not forsake us
but faithfully intercedes for us
as she stands with her Son in glory.
Blessed be Mary, Virgin and Mother!
~AMEN.

READING   VICTORY OVER DEATH   1 CORINTHIANS 15:54–57

"Death has been swallowed up in victory. Where, O death, is your victory? Where, O death, is your sting?" The sting of death is sin, and the power of sin is the law. But thanks be to God, who gives us the victory through our Lord Jesus Christ.

SILENCE

RESPONSE

The holy Mother of God is exalted, alleluia!
~ABOVE THE CHOIRS OF ANGELS, ALLELUIA!

TE MATREM LAUDAMUS

We praise you as our Mother,
we acclaim you as our blessed Lady.
All the earth reveres you,
the daughter of the Eternal Father.

The hosts of heaven and all the angelic powers
sing your praise:
the angels join in the dance,
the archangels applaud, the virtues give praise,
the principalities rejoice, the powers exult,
the dominations delight, the thrones make
festival,
the cherubim and seraphim cry out unceasingly:

Holy, holy, holy is the great Mother of God,
Mary most holy;
the blessed fruit of your womb
is the glory of heaven and earth.

The glorious choir of apostles,
the noble company of prophets,
the white-robed army of martyrs,
all sing your praise.

The holy Church throughout the world celebrates
you:
the daughter of infinite Majesty,
the mother of God's true and only Son,
the bride of the Spirit of truth and consolation.

You bore Christ, the King of glory,
the eternal Son of the Father.
When he took our flesh to set us free,
he humbly chose your virgin womb.

When he overcame death's sting,
he assumed you into heaven.

You now sit with your Son
at God's right hand in glory.
Intercede for us, O Virgin Mary,
when he comes to be our judge.

Help your chosen people
bought with Christ's precious blood.
And bring us with all the saints
to glory everlasting.[53]

NOVENA PRAYER

We turn to you for protection,
holy Mother of God.
Listen to our prayers
and help us in our needs.
(Here we state our needs.)
Save us from every danger,
glorious and blessed Virgin.[54]

May the Queen of all saints
✝ intercede for us with the Lord.
~AMEN.

Novenas to the Saints

A Novena to St. John the Baptist

It was John's mission—and greatness—to pro-claim the advent of the kingdom of God. Nor was he in any way unworthy to do so, he who even from his mother's womb (Luke 1:15) was filled with the Holy Spirit. It could only mean that it was his particular vocation to lead the way to the promised realm, to direct others to it, but in some special way to remain outside it. One is reminded of Moses close to death, standing on Mount Nebo and looking down on the Promised Land. He was not allowed to enter. Not until he has passed through death does he come into the true land of promise. For Moses this was punish-ment; he had failed in an hour of trial. For John it was not punishment but vocation. . . . This side of death, John was to remain Precursor: herald of the kingdom.[55]

In North America, the Baptist is the special patron of French Canada.

There was a man sent from God
~WHOSE NAME WAS JOHN.

Many will rejoice at John's birth,
~FOR HE WILL BE FILLED WITH THE HOLY SPIRIT.

Among those born of women
~NO ONE HAS ARISEN GREATER THAN JOHN THE
    BAPTIST.

HYMN

God called great prophets to foretell
The coming of his Son;
The greatest, called before his birth,
Was John, the chosen one.

John searched in solitude for Christ,
And knew him when he came;
He showed the world the Lamb of God,
And hailed him in our name.

That lonely voice cried out in truth,
Derided and denied;
As witness to the law of God
His mighty martyr died.

We praise you, Trinity in One,
The light of unknown ways,
The hope of all who search for you,
Whose love fills all our days.[56]

PSALM 146   GOD KEEPS FAITH

ANTIPHON John was not himself the light
BUT CAME TO TESTIFY TO THE LIGHT.

Praise the Lord, O my soul!
I will praise the Lord as long as I live;
I will sing praises to my God while I have life.

Do not put your trust in rulers,
in mortals, in whom there is no help.
Their breath departs, they return to the earth;
on that very day their plans perish.

Happy are those whose help is in the God of
   Jacob,
whose hope is in the Lord, their God,
who made heaven and earth,
the sea, and all that is in them;
who keeps faith for ever;
who executes justice for the oppressed;
who gives food to the hungry.

The Lord sets the prisoners free;
the Lord opens the eyes of the blind.
The Lord lifts up those who are bowed down;
the Lord loves the righteous.

The Lord watches over the aliens,
and upholds the widow and the orphan;
but the Lord brings the way of the wicked to ruin.
The Lord will reign for ever,
from generation to generation.

ANTIPHON JOHN HIMSELF WAS NOT THE LIGHT
BUT CAME TO TESTIFY TO THE LIGHT.

Psalm Prayer

Let us pray *(pause for quiet prayer):*

Righteous God,
you raised up John the Baptist,
a fearless and outspoken prophet,
to prepare the way for Jesus your Son.
Make us listen to his message of repentance
and have a change of heart
to prepare a welcome for the reign of God
that comes to us in Jesus the Messiah,
who lives and reigns for ever and ever.
~Amen.

Reading   John the Forerunner   Isaiah 40:3–5

A voice cries out: "In the wilderness prepare the way of the Lord, make straight in the desert a highway for our God. Every valley shall be lifted up, and every mountain and hill be made low; the uneven ground shall become level, and the rough places a plain. Then the glory of the Lord shall be revealed."

Silence

Response

Among those born of women
~No one is greater than John the Baptist.

Canticle of Zachary   Luke 1:68–79[57]

Antiphon An angel of the Lord appeared to Zachary, standing at the right side of the altar of incense.

Blessed are you, ✝ Lord, the God of Israel,
you have come to your people and set them free.
You have raised up for us a mighty Savior,
born of the house of your servant David.

Through your holy prophets, you promised of old
    to save us from our enemies,
    from the hands of all who hate us,
    to show mercy to our forebears,
    and to remember your holy covenant.

This was the oath you swore to our father
    Abraham:
    to set us free from the hands of our enemies,
    free to worship you without fear,
    holy and righteous before you,
    all the days of our life.

And you, child, shall be called the prophet of the
    Most High,
for you will go before the Lord to prepare the way,
to give God's people knowledge of salvation
by the forgiveness of their sins.

In the tender compassion of our God
the dawn from on high shall break upon us,
to shine on those who dwell in darkness
    and the shadow of death,
and to guide our feet into the way of peace.

Glory to the Holy and Undivided Trinity:
now and always and for ever and ever. Amen.

ANTIPHON AN ANGEL OF THE LORD APPEARED TO ZACHARY, STANDING AT THE RIGHT SIDE OF THE ALTAR OF INCENSE.

LITANY

In memory of John the Forerunner
    and his call to repentance, we pray:
~LORD, HAVE MERCY.

For prophets who fearlessly proclaim the truth
    to the Church and the world, we pray:
~LORD, HAVE MERCY.

For a true change of heart and a steadfast spirit,
    we pray:
~LORD, HAVE MERCY.

For preachers who are the salt of the earth
    and the light of the world, we pray:
~LORD, HAVE MERCY.

For the preaching of sound doctrine, in season
    and out of season, we pray:
~LORD, HAVE MERCY.

For the communion of holy things and holy
    people, we pray:
~LORD, HAVE MERCY.

For all who have died in the peace of Christ, we pray:
~LORD, HAVE MERCY.

(Pause for spontaneous petitions.)

For the prayers of the Blessed Virgin Mary, of
   John the Baptist, prophet and martyr, and of
   Zachary and Elizabeth, his parents:
~LORD, HAVE MERCY.

PRAYER
Almighty God,
you called John the Baptist
to give witness to the coming of your Son
and to prepare his way.
Give the people the wisdom to see your purpose,
and the openness to do your will,
that we too may witness to Christ's coming
and so prepare his way;
through your Son Jesus Christ our Lord,
who lives and reigns with you and the Holy Spirit,
one God, now and for ever.
~AMEN.[58]

May the Word made flesh, full of grace and truth,
✝ bless us and keep us.
~AMEN.

A Novena to
St. Joseph of Nazareth

St. Joseph played an important role in the infancy and
childhood of Jesus. As a righteous and obedient servant
of God, he accepted and supported Mary, his pregnant
fiancée; guided her from Nazareth to Bethlehem; found
a place for them to stay; arranged Jesus' circumcision
and name-day ceremony; accompanied Mary to Jesus'

presentation in the temple; went into exile with Jesus and Mary; and when Jesus was twelve years old, found him again in the temple. Joseph earned a living for the holy family as a workman, possibly as a carpenter, and is the special patron saint of those who work with their hands. He is also the patron of the Universal Church and of the dying.

His central shrine in North America is the Oratory of St. Joseph, founded in Montreal, Quebec, by the miracle worker Blessed Andre Bessette, CSC (1845–1937).

In the name of the Father, † and of the Son, and of the Holy Spirit.
~AMEN.

HYMN

Joseph, we praise you, prince of God's own
    household,
Hearing the promise made of old to David,
Chosen to foster Christ, the Lord's anointed,
Son of the Father.

Strong in your silence, swift in your obedience,
Saving God's firstborn, when you fled from Herod,
Cherish God's children as you cherished Jesus,
Safe in your keeping.

Husband of Mary, one in joy and sorrow,
share with God's people love and peace and
    blessing;
may your example help our homes to mirror
Nazareth's glory.

Saint of the dying, when your work was ended
Jesus and Mary stood beside your deathbed;
so in life's evening may they stand beside you,
calling us homeward.[59]

PSALM 92:1–5, 12–15   JOSEPH THE JUST

ANTIPHON   The righteous flourish like the palm
    tree, AND GROW LIKE A CEDAR IN LEBANON.

It is good to give thanks to the Lord,
to sing praises to your name, O Most High;
to declare your steadfast love in the morning,
and your faithfulness by night,
to the music of the lute and the harp,
to the melody of the lyre.

For you, O Lord, have made me glad by your
    works;
at the works of your hands I sing for joy.
How great are your works, O Lord!
Your thoughts are very deep!

The righteous flourish like the palm tree,
and grow like a cedar in Lebanon.
They are planted in the house of the Lord,
they flourish in the courts of our God.

Still productive in old age,
they are full of sap and green,
showing that the Lord is upright.
The Lord is my rock
in whom there is no unrighteousness.

ANTIPHON THE RIGHTEOUS FLOURISH LIKE THE
PALM TREE, AND GROW LIKE A CEDAR IN
LEBANON.

PSALM PRAYER

Let us pray *(pause for quiet prayer):*

God of the righteous,
you guided holy Joseph by angels
and made him the protector of the holy family
at Bethlehem, in Egypt, and at Nazareth.
By your eternal love for us,
make him our guide and protector in this life
and especially at the hour of our death.
We ask this through Christ our Lord.
~AMEN.

READING JOSEPH AND MARY MATTHEW 1:18–21

When Jesus' mother Mary had been engaged to
Joseph, but before they lived together, she was
found to be with child from the Holy Spirit.
Her husband Joseph, being a righteous man
and unwilling to expose her to public disgrace,
planned to dismiss her quietly. But just when
he had resolved to do this, an angel of the Lord
appeared to him in a dream and said, "Joseph,
son of David, do not be afraid to take Mary as
your wife, for the child conceived in her is from
the Holy Spirit. She will bear a son, and you are to

name him Jesus, for he will save his people from their sins."

SILENCE

RESPONSE
Jesus was, in the eyes of the law,
~THE SON OF JOSEPH.

LITANY OF ST. JOSEPH (SEE PAGES 255–257)

NOVENA PRAYER
Good St. Joseph,
faithful guardian of the holy family,
protect the chosen people of Jesus Christ
and be our ally in our conflict
with the powers of darkness.
As you rescued the child Jesus from Herod,
defend now the Universal Church from all harm.
Please listen to our prayers
and help us in all our needs.
(Here we state our needs.)
By your help and example,
may we lead a holy life, die a godly death,
and attain to a blessed eternity in heaven.
~AMEN.

May Jesus, the son of Joseph,
✝ bless us and keep us.
~AMEN.

A Novena to the Archangels Michael, Gabriel, and Raphael

Lest we forget the mighty beings whom God created before the race of humans and their care for us, we call to mind the three princes of the heavenly host—Michael, Gabriel, and Raphael—who surround and protect the people of God. Like all angels they are pure spirits whom God puts at the service of Christ and his Church. Throughout the Bible, they act as divine messengers to God's chosen ones and will accompany Christ when he comes in glory to judge the living and the dead. Their common feast day is September 29.

The Beauty of Angels

By the same light [of grace] the soul can see spiritually the beauty of angels and their dignity by nature: the subtlety of their substance, their confirmation in grace, the fullness of their eternal glory, the diversity of their orders, and the distinction of their persons; how they live all in the light of eternal truth, and how they burn all in love of the Holy Spirit according to the dignity of their orders; how they see, love and praise Jesus in blessed rest, without ceasing. In this kind of work there is no vision of the body or of a figure of the imagination, but all is spiritual, and concerning spiritual creatures.

Then the soul begins to have a great acquaintance with these blessed spirits, and a great fellowship; for they are very tender towards such a soul, and busy themselves in helping it; they are masters to teach it, and through their spiritual presence and the touching of their light they often drive out phantoms from the soul,

which they illuminate through grace. They com-
fort the soul with sweet words quickly uttered
in a pure heart, and if it meets with any spiritual
distress they serve the soul and administer all
that it needs. . . . No tongue can tell the particu-
lar feelings, illuminations, graces and comforts
that pure souls perceive through the fellowship
and favor of blessed angels.[60]

In the presence of the angels I will bless you.
~I WILL ADORE YOU BEFORE YOUR HOLY TEMPLE.

An angel with a golden censer
~CAME AND STOOD AT THE HEAVENLY ALTAR.

The smoke of the incense rose before God
~WITH THE PRAYERS OF THE SAINTS.

HYMN

Christ, you are the Father's splendor,
Over earth and heaven king;
In the presence of the angels,
Here your rightful praise we sing
Duly in alternate chorus,
That our homage we may bring.

Thus we praise with veneration
All archangels round your throne;
Praising first their leader, Michael,
Heavenly guardian of your own,
Who in princely virtue banished
Satan to the realms unknown.

By his watchful care repelling
In the power of your grace,

Every unseen adversary,
All things evil, all things base.
Grant us, Savior, of your goodness,
In your paradise a place.

Glory be to God and honor
To the Father and the Son,
And with them the Holy Spirit,
Ever Three and ever One,
Who with joy fills all creation
While unending ages run.[61]

Psalm 150   THE ANGELIC ANTHEM

ANTIPHON Bless the Lord, O angels,
YOU MIGHTY ONES WHO DO GOD'S BIDDING.

Praise God in the sanctuary;
praise God in the mighty firmament!
Praise God for mighty deeds;
praise God for exceeding greatness!

Praise God with trumpet sound;
praise God with lute and harp!
Praise God with tambourine and dance;
praise God with strings and pipe!

Praise God with sounding cymbals;
praise God with loud clashing cymbals!
Let everything that breathes praise the Lord!
Praise the Lord!

ANTIPHON BLESS THE LORD, O ANGELS,
YOU MIGHTY ONES WHO DO GOD'S BIDDING.

PSALM PRAYER

Let us pray *(pause for quiet prayer)*:

Lord God almighty,
you created both angels and humans
to worship and serve you.
May your holy angels protect us
and defend us against every evil.
In Jesus' name we ask it.
~AMEN.

	GUARDIAN	MATTHEW
READING	ANGELS	18:1–3, 10

The disciples came to Jesus and asked, "Who is
the greatest in the kingdom of heaven?" He called
a child, whom he put among them, and said,
"Truly I tell you, unless you change and become
like children, you will never enter the kingdom
of heaven. Take care that you do not despise one
of these little ones; for, I tell you, in heaven their
angels continually see the face of my Father in
heaven."

SILENCE

RESPONSE

Holy Michael the Archangel, defend us in battle
~THAT WE MAY NOT PERISH ON THE DAY OF
   JUDGMENT.

CANTICLE OF A JOYFUL ASSEMBLY HEBREWS 12:22–24, 28

ANTIPHON The angel Gabriel said to Mary, "YOU WILL CONCEIVE AND BEAR A SON, AND YOU WILL NAME HIM JESUS."

We have come to Mount Zion
and to the city of the living God,
the heavenly Jerusalem,
and to innumerable angels in festal gathering.

We have come to the assembly of the firstborn
who are enrolled in heaven,
and to God the judge of all,
and to the spirits of the righteous made perfect,
and to Jesus, the mediator of a new covenant,
and to the sprinkled blood that speaks a better
    word
than the blood of Abel.

Since we are receiving a kingdom
that cannot be shaken,
let us give thanks,
by which we offer to God an acceptable worship
with reverence and awe;
for indeed our God is a consuming fire.

Glory to God: Father, Son, and Holy Spirit:
now and always and for ever and ever. Amen.

ANTIPHON THE ANGEL GABRIEL SAID TO MARY, "YOU WILL CONCEIVE AND BEAR A SON, AND YOU WILL NAME HIM JESUS."

LITANY

With the whole company of heaven, we pray:

~LORD, HEAR OUR PRAYER.

With the prayers of Michael the Archangel,
who vanquished Lucifer from the courts of
heaven:

~LORD, HEAR OUR PRAYER.

With the prayers of Gabriel the Archangel,
who brought the good news to Mary and
Joseph:

~LORD, HEAR OUR PRAYER.

With the prayers of Raphael the Archangel,
who healed the sick and guided the lost:

~LORD, HEAR OUR PRAYER.

With the help of our guardian angels
who watch over and protect us:

~LORD, HEAR OUR PRAYER.

With the sick, the dying, and all the faithful
departed:

~LORD, HEAR OUR PRAYER.

(Pause for spontaneous petitions.)

With the prayers of Our Lady of the Angels, the
Queen of heaven, and of all the angels and
saints:

~LORD, HEAR OUR PRAYER.

PRAYER

Gracious God,
you have established the nine orders of angels
to reflect your glory and majesty
and to keep watch over your chosen people.
May Michael, the prince of the heavenly host,
Gabriel, the celestial messenger,
and Raphael, the healer of souls and bodies,
be the ever watchful guardians of your Church
and your messengers in time of need.
We ask this through Christ, Lord of the angels.
~Amen.

Blessing and glory and wisdom and thanksgiving
and honor and power and might
✝ be to our God, for ever and ever.
~Amen.

A Novena to St. Francis of Assisi

St. Francis is everybody's saint. For believers he is the very incarnation of the gospel, the one who imitated Christ literally and perfectly. Francis drew companions to himself and founded the Little Brothers of the Gospel to proclaim Christ throughout the world. He and St. Clare also founded the Poor Ladies of Assisi, a cloistered order of women vowed to the same poverty and humility as the Brothers. Later, Francis drew laypeople into the Order of Penance to bring about a spiritual and moral change in the family and in society. He especially charged them not to carry weapons, not to participate in war, but instead to be peacemakers.

Two years before he died in 1226, Francis received the sacred stigmata in his hands, feet, and side to mark him for all time as a living icon of the Crucified. Like Jesus and with Jesus himself, he stands with uplifted and pierced hands before the throne of God to make intercession for us in all our needs. He is the special friend of the poor and disheartened, those suffering from oppression, and of a world in need of peace.

In the name of the Father, † and of the Son, and of the Holy Spirit.
~AMEN.

Bless the Lord, sing to God's glory,
~ALL THINGS FASHIONED BY GOD'S MIGHTY HAND.

HYMN

Most high, omnipotent, good Lord,
To you be ceaseless praise outpoured,
From you alone all creatures came;
No one is worthy you to name.

My Lord, be praised by Brother Sun
Who through the skies his course does run:
With brightness he does fill the day,
And signifies your boundless sway.

By Sister Moon, my Lord, be praised,
With all the stars in heaven arrayed,
Let wind and air, and cloud and calm,
And weathers let repeat the psalm.

By Sister Water, then be blessed:
Most humble, useful, precious, chaste.
Be praised by Brother Fire, so bright
Who lightens, cheerfully, the night.

My Lord, be praised by Mother Earth,
From whom all living things take birth:
Sustained by you through every hour,
She brings forth fruit and herb and flower.

My Lord, be praised by those who prove
In free forgivingness their love.
Blest are all those who trials endure
For you, O Lord: their hope is sure.

By Death, our sister, praised be:
From her your people cannot flee.
Most blest are those who do your will,
And follow your commandments still.

Most high, omnipotent, good Lord,
To you be ceaseless praise outpoured;
Let every creature thankful be
And serve in great humility.[62]

PSALM 142   FRANCIS' DEATHBED PSALM

ANTIPHON Bring me out of prison,
SO THAT I MAY GIVE THANKS TO YOUR NAME!

With my voice I cry to the Lord,
I make supplication;
Before the Lord I tell my trouble,
I pour out my complaint.

When my spirit is faint,
you know my way.

In the path where I walk
they have hidden a trap for me.
Look on my right hand and see;
there is no one who takes notice of me;
no refuge remains for me,
no one cares for me.

I cry to you, O Lord;
I say, "You are my refuge,
my portion in the land of the living."
Give heed to my cry;
for I am brought very low.

Save me from my persecutors;
for they are too strong for me.
Bring me out of prison,
so that I may give thanks to your name!
The righteous will surround me,
for you will deal richly with me.

ANTIPHON BRING ME OUT OF PRISON,
SO THAT I MAY GIVE THANKS TO YOUR NAME!

PSALM PRAYER

Let us pray *(pause for quiet prayer)*:

Lord God,
you guided Francis along the path
of voluntary poverty and peacemaking
and brought his soul out of prison
that he might fully praise you.

By his example and prayers,
form us according to the gospel of Jesus,
who ransomed us with his precious blood.
We ask this through the same Christ our Lord.
~Amen.

The Stigmata

Reading   Galatians 6:14, 17

May I never boast of anything except the cross
of our Lord Jesus Christ, by which the world has
been crucified to me, and I to the world. From
now on, let no one make trouble for me; for I
carry the marks of Jesus branded on my body.

Silence

Response
Blessed are the peacemakers,
~For they will be called the children of
  God.

Canticle of Praise of St. Francis of Assisi
Holy, holy, holy, the Lord God the Almighty,
who was and who is and who is to come.
~Let us praise and exalt our God for ever!

Worthy are you, O Lord our God,
to receive praise and glory, honor and blessing.
~Let us praise and exalt our God for ever!

Worthy is the Lamb who was slain
to receive power and divinity, wisdom and might,
and honor and glory and blessing.
~Let us praise and exalt our God for ever!

Let us bless the Father and the Son with the Holy
Spirit.

~Let us praise and exalt our God for ever!

Bless the Lord, sing to God's glory,
all things fashioned by God's mighty hand.

~Let us praise and exalt our God for ever!

Sing praise to God, all you people of God,
who stand in awe of God, both small and great.

~Let us praise and exalt our God for ever!

Let heaven and earth praise the Glorious One:
every creature in heaven and on earth,
under the earth and in the sea, and all that is in
them.

~Let us praise and exalt our God for ever!

Glory to the Father and to the Son and to the Holy
Spirit:

~Let us praise and exalt our God for ever!

As it was in the beginning, is now, and will be for
ever. Amen.

~Let us praise and exalt our God for ever![63]

LITANY

By the example of the poor little man of Assisi,

~Teach us the values of poverty and
simplicity.

By his devotion to the cross and the wounds of Jesus,

~Teach us to venerate the five holy
wounds.

By the devotion of Francis to the Holy Eucharist,
~Teach us to adore the Sacrament of the
Altar.

By the devotion Francis practiced to Our Lady of
the Angels,
~Teach us to love our Blessed Mother.

By the love and commitment of Francis to the
Daily Office,
~Teach us to pray in season and out of
season.

By the respect Francis had for priests,
~Teach us to respect their office and
their gifts.

By the affectionate respect Francis and Clare
had for each other,
~Teach us to value enduring Christian
friendship.

By the insight Francis gained from the Bible and
from nature,
~Teach us to read them both with him.

(Here we state our needs.)

By the intercession of Our Lady of the Angels, of
St. Francis and St. Clare, and of all the saints,
~Teach us to cherish the communion of
saints.

PRAYER

Lord Jesus Christ,
as the world was growing cold,
you renewed the marks of your five wounds
in the flesh of your servant Francis
in order to warm our cold hearts again.
By these signs of love made visible,
may we be inspired to walk with him
the royal road of the cross
until we reach our heavenly home,
where you live and reign with your Father
and the holy and life-giving Spirit,
for ever and ever.
~AMEN.

May the LORD ✝ bless us and take care of us.
~AMEN.

May the LORD be kind and gracious to us.
~AMEN.

May the LORD look on us with favor
    and give us peace.
~AMEN.

A Novena to
Padre Pio of Pietrelcina

Padre Pio is one of the most renowned sons of St. Francis of Assisi and the first priest in history to be marked, like Francis himself, with the five wounds of Jesus. He came from an Italian peasant background (born in 1887) and spent most of his life in an obscure Capuchin Franciscan friary in the small town of San Giovanni Rotondo. From 1910 (the year of his ordination) until a few months before he died in 1968, he suffered severely from the stigmata in his hands, feet, and side. His ministry was marked by devotion to the sick and the poor and was invested with the gifts of prophecy and the ability to read consciences and perform exemplary miracles of healing. He suffered not only from the wounds in his hands, feet, and side but also from the unrelenting pressure of pilgrims and penitents who besieged him day in and day out. Padre Pio was beatified by Pope John Paul II in 1999 and canonized on June 16, 2002.

You, Christ, are the King of glory,
~THE ETERNAL SON OF THE FATHER.

You overcame the sting of death
~AND OPENED THE KINGDOM OF HEAVEN TO ALL
BELIEVERS.

HYMN
At the name of Jesus
Every knee should bow,
Every tongue confess him
King of glory now;
'Tis the Father's pleasure
We should call him Lord,
Who from the beginning
Was the mighty Word.

Mighty and mysterious
In the highest height,

God from everlasting,
Very light of light:
In the Father's bosom
With the Spirit blest,
Love, in love eternal,
Rest, in perfect rest.

Humbled for a season,
To receive a name
From the lips of sinners
Unto whom he came,
Faithfully he bore it
Spotless to the last,
Brought it back victorious
When from death he passed.[64]

PSALM 67   IN THE CROSS IS VICTORY

ANTIPHON Let us glory in the cross of our Lord
Jesus Christ.

IN HIM IS OUR SALVATION, LIFE, AND
RESURRECTION, ALLELUIA!

O God, be gracious to us and bless us
and make your face to shine upon us,
that your way may be known upon earth,
your saving power among all nations.

Let the peoples praise you, O God,
let all the peoples praise you!

Let the nations be glad and sing for joy,
for you judge the peoples with equity
and guide the nations upon earth.

Let the peoples praise you, O God,
let all the peoples praise you!

The earth has yielded its increase;
God, our God, has blessed us.
May God bless us;
let all the ends of the earth fear God!

Let the peoples praise you, O God,
let all the peoples praise you!

ANTIPHON LET US GLORY IN THE CROSS OF OUR
LORD JESUS CHRIST.
IN HIM IS OUR SALVATION, LIFE, AND
RESURRECTION, ALLELUIA!

PSALM PRAYER

Let us pray *(pause for quiet prayer):*

Lord Jesus Christ,
by the precious wounds
in your hands, feet, and side,
be gracious to us and bless us
and make your saving power known
among all nations,
now and for ever.
~AMEN.

	THE YOKE OF	**MATTHEW**
READING	**CHRIST JESUS**	**11:28–30**

"Come to me, all you that are weary and are
carrying heavy burdens, and I will give you rest.
Take my yoke upon you, and learn from me; for I
am gentle and humble in heart, and you will find

rest for your souls. For my yoke is easy, and my burden is light."

SILENCE

RESPONSE
I have been crucified with Christ,
~AND CHRIST LIVES IN ME.

CANTICLE OF ST. FRANCIS OF ASSISI
Most High, Almighty, good Lord!
We praise, glorify, honor, and exalt you!
Your name is above all names
and is the delight of heaven and earth.
~WE PRAISE YOU, O LORD!

Praise to you, O Lord our God,
for all you have created:
first, for the Sun, our Brother,
who gives us the light of day
as he shines in radiant splendor,
in your very likeness, O Lord.
~WE PRAISE YOU, O LORD!

We praise you for the Moon, our Sister,
and for the bright, flashing stars of heaven:
~WE PRAISE YOU, O LORD!

We praise you for the Wind, our Brother,
for fair and stormy days and seasons
by which you nourish and refresh
all that you have made:
~WE PRAISE YOU, O LORD!

We praise you for Water, our Sister,
so useful, simple, precious, and pure:
~WE PRAISE YOU, O LORD!

We praise you for the Fire, our Brother,
who illumines our darkest nights
with radiant light, both physical and spiritual:
~WE PRAISE YOU, O LORD!

We praise you for our Mother Earth,
who supports and feeds us,
giving us our food in due season:
~WE PRAISE YOU, O LORD!

We praise you, O Most High,
for those who forgive one another
     for love of you,
and who patiently bear life's trials and
     tribulations.
You will crown those, O Lord, who patiently
     endure.
~WE PRAISE YOU, O LORD!

We praise you for our Sister Death,
the unavoidable fact of life.
Happy are those she finds doing God's will!
The Second Death has no hold on them:
~WE PRAISE YOU, O LORD!

All creatures, fashioned by God's mighty hand,
praise, glorify, and thank our Creator
and serve the Lord in great humility:
~WE PRAISE YOU, O LORD![65]

Litany of the Precious Blood
(see pages 248–251)

Novena Prayer

Lord Jesus Crucified,
you raised up your servant Padre Pio
and marked him with your five precious wounds
to recall us to your sufferings and death on the
    cross.
By his example of faith and fervor,
may we be rescued from all our sins
and brought into submission to your holy will
and by his loving intercession
may we lay our needs before you in full trust.
(Here we state our needs.)
Blessed Savior,
by the prayers of Padre Pio and of all your saints.
make us fit to reign with you for ever and ever.
~Amen.

May the Lord ✝ bless us and take care of us.
~Amen.

May the Lord be kind and gracious to us.
~Amen.

May the Lord look on us with favor
    and give us peace.
~Amen.

Novena to St. Anthony of Padua

Anthony of Padua (1195–1231) was a Portuguese priest and canon who transferred to the Franciscans in 1221 while St. Francis was still alive. Learned, zealous, and persuasive, Anthony became one of the most renowned preachers of his time, contributing to a moral reformation in the cities of France and Italy. He was also very successful in converting heretics and in assisting the poor and helpless. Pope Gregory IX, who heard him preach, called him "the living repository of the Holy Scriptures." In the Order he was the first teacher of theology, a minister provincial, a renowned preacher of the Assumption of our Lady, and was regarded by St. Francis as his "bishop" during the last six years of his life. Worn out by his labors, he died prematurely on June 13, 1231 at the age of thirty-six. He was canonized the following year and declared a Doctor of the Church by Pope Pius XII in 1946. He is called the "Wonder-worker" because of his many miracles, and "Friend of the Poor" because of his love and care of the poor, the neglected, and the oppressed. In Catholic folklore, people pray to him for the return of lost articles.

In the name of the Father, ✝ and of the Son,
and of the Holy Spirit.
~Amen.

Light shines forth for the just
~And joy for the upright of heart.

Hymn

This is the feast of the Lord's true witness,
Whom through the ages all have held in honor;
Now let us praise him and his deeds of glory

With exultation.

So now together, giving God the glory,
We sing his praises and his mighty triumph,
That in his glory we may all be sharers,
Now and hereafter.

Praise to the Father and the Son most holy,
Praise to the Spirit, Godhead coeternal,
Who give examples in the lives of all saints,
That we may follow.[66]

PSALM 144:1–6, 9–10   GOD'S SERVANT

ANTIPHON Happy are the people WHOSE GOD IS
THE LORD.

Blessed be the Lord, my rock,
who trains my hands for war,
and my fingers for battle;
my rock and my fortress,
my stronghold and my deliverer,
my shield in whom I take refuge,
who subdues the peoples under me.

O Lord, what are human beings that you regard
them,
or mortals that you think of them?
They are like a breath,
their days are like a passing shadow.

Bow your heavens, O Lord, and come down.
Touch the mountains so that they smoke.
Make the lightning flash and scatter them;
send out your arrows and rout them.

I will sing you a new song, O God;
I will play the harp and sing to you.
You give victory to kings
and rescue your servant David.

ANTIPHON HAPPY ARE THE PEOPLE WHOSE GOD
IS THE LORD.

PSALM PRAYER

Let us pray *(pause for quiet prayer):*

True and deathless God,
may our remembrance of St. Anthony,
devoted preacher and doctor of the church,
give us joy in believing and zeal in observing
the sound truths of the holy Catholic Church.
We ask this through Christ our Lord.
~AMEN.

SALT
READING **AND LIGHT** **MATTHEW 5:14–16**

"You are the light of the world. A city built on a hill
cannot be hid. No one after lighting a lamp puts it
under the bushel basket, but on the lampstand, and it
gives light to all in the house. In the same way, let your
light shine before others, so that they may see your
good works and give glory to your Father in heaven."

SILENCE

RESPONSE

Blessed are the peacemakers,
~FOR THEY WILL BE CALLED THE CHILDREN OF
GOD.

CANTICLE OF THE
BLESSED VIRGIN MARY
LUKE 1:46–55[67]

ANTIPHON Blessed be the great Mother of God,
MARY MOST HOLY,
WHO WAS ASSUMED BODY AND SOUL INTO
HEAVEN, ALLELUIA!

My soul † proclaims the greatness of the Lord,
my spirit rejoices in God my Savior,
for you, Lord, have looked with favor on your
lowly servant.

From this day all generations will call me blessed:
you, the Almighty, have done great things for me
and holy is your name.
You have mercy on those who fear you,
from generation to generation.

You have shown strength with your arm
and scattered the proud in their conceit,
casting down the mighty from their thrones
and lifting up the lowly.
You have filled the hungry with good things
and sent the rich away empty.

You have come to the aid of your servant Israel,
to remember the promise of mercy,
the promise made to our forebears,
to Abraham and his children for ever.

Glory to the Father, and to the Son,
and to the Holy Spirit:
as it was in the beginning, is now,
and will be for ever. Amen.

A Novena to St. Anthony of Padua **147**

ANTIPHON BLESSED BE THE GREAT MOTHER OF
GOD, MARY MOST HOLY,
WHO WAS ASSUMED BODY AND SOUL INTO
HEAVEN, ALLELUIA!

LITANY

For the one, holy, catholic, and apostolic Church,
of all peoples everywhere, let us pray to the
Lord.

~LORD, HAVE MERCY.

For our bishops, priests, and deacons, and for all
who serve God in the true faith, let us pray to
the Lord.

~LORD, HAVE MERCY.

For the peace that comes from heaven and for the
union of all churches, let us pray to the Lord.

~LORD, HAVE MERCY.

For fervent preachers of the holy gospel,
in season and out of season, let us pray to the
Lord.

~LORD, HAVE MERCY.

For the rulers of the earth to maintain justice and
peace in this world, let us pray to the Lord.

~LORD, HAVE MERCY.

For the fruits of the earth, for the sowing and the
harvest, and for the poor who set their hope in
God, let us pray to the Lord.

~LORD, HAVE MERCY.

For those who have fallen asleep in Christ,
    especially *Names,* let us pray to the Lord.
~LORD, HAVE MERCY.

For those whom we call to mind today, *Names,*
    let us pray to the Lord.
~LORD, HAVE MERCY.

For a part and inheritance in the glorious company
    of Mary most holy, of St. Anthony the Wonder-
    worker, and of all the saints, let us pray to the
    Lord.
~LORD, HAVE MERCY.

NOVENA PRAYER

Lord Jesus Christ,
faithful preacher of the Good News,
we thank you for raising up Anthony of Padua
who proclaimed peace and reconciliation
in season and out of season.
By his example and prayers,
shape us in sound praying
as we present our needs before you.
(Here we state our needs.)
Please give us convincing preachers in our time
who will stir our hearts and minds
to love and observe the holy gospel
without fear or failing.
You live and reign, now and for ever.
~AMEN.

May the divine assistance ✝ remain always with
us.
~Amen.

A Novena to St. Jude the Apostle

Although the least known of the twelve apostles, Jude
left us one of the New Testament letters. In it he refers
to himself as "Jude/Judas, a servant of Jesus Christ
and the brother of James," the Righteous, that is,
"James the Lord's brother," as he is called in Galatians
1:19. He writes mostly to rebuke those who attack and
undermine "the faith that once for all was entrusted
to the saints" (verse 3). He concludes by exhorting
his hearers "to build yourselves up on your most
holy faith; pray in the Holy Spirit; keep yourselves
in the love of God. . . . and have mercy on some
who are wavering" (verses 20–22). He is believed to
have been martyred in Persia along with St. Simon
the Zealot/Canaanite. They share a feast day in the
Roman calendar on October 28.

He is known as "the saint of impossible cases" and
is often invoked accordingly.

In the name of the Father, ✝ and of the Son,
and of the Holy Spirit.
~Amen.

I am a witness of Christ's sufferings
~And I will share in the glory that will
be revealed.

Hymn

Soldiers of Christ, arise,
And put your armor on,
Strong in the strength that God supplies
Through his eternal Son;
Strong in the Lord of Hosts,
And in his mighty power,
Who in the strength of Jesus trusts
Is more than conqueror.

Stand then in his great might,
With all his strength endued;
But take, to arm you for the fight,
The panoply of God;
That having all things done,
And all your conflicts past,
You may overcome through Christ alone,
And stand entire at last.[68]

Psalm 66:1–4, 8–9, 16–17, 20   Thanksgiving

Antiphon Blessed be God WHO HAS NOT
REJECTED MY PRAYER.

Make a joyful noise to God, all the earth;
sing the glory of God's name;
give to God glorious praise!
Say to God, "How awesome are your deeds!
Because of your great power,
your enemies cringe before you.

All the earth worships you;
they sing praises to you,
sing praises to your name."

Bless our God, O peoples,
let the sound of God's praise be heard,
who has kept us among the living
and has not let our foot slip.

Come and hear, all you who worship God,
and I will tell what God has done for me.
I cried aloud to God,
who was highly praised with my tongue.

If I had cherished iniquity in my heart,
the Lord would not have listened.
But truly God has listened,
and has given heed to the voice of my prayer.
Blessed be God, who has not rejected my prayer
or removed his steadfast love from me.

ANTIPHON BLESSED BE GOD WHO HAS NOT
 REJECTED MY PRAYER.

PSALM PRAYER

Let us pray *(pause for quiet prayer)*:
God of truth and mercy,
may we cry out with your holy apostles:
"How awesome are your deeds!"
With Jude, who contended for the faith
that was entrusted to the saints once for all,
may high praise be ready on our tongues,
through the merits of Christ our Savior.
~AMEN.

You, beloved, must remember the predictions
of the apostles of our Lord Jesus Christ; for
they said to you, "In the last time there will be
scoffers, indulging their own ungodly lusts." It
is these worldly people, devoid of the Spirit, who
are causing divisions. But you, beloved, build
yourselves up on your most holy faith; pray in the
Holy Spirit; keep yourselves in the love of God;
look forward to the mercy of our Lord Jesus Christ
that leads to eternal life.

SILENCE

RESPONSE

The LORD comes to rule the earth,

~COMES WITH JUSTICE TO RULE THE WORLD.

CANTICLE OF REVELATION (1:4–8)

ANTIPHON "I am the Alpha and the Omega,"

WHO IS AND WHO WAS AND WHO IS TO COME,

   THE ALMIGHTY.

Grace to you and peace
from him who is and who was
and who is to come,
and from Jesus Christ, the faithful witness,
the firstborn of the dead,
and the ruler of the kings of the earth.

To Christ who loves us
and freed us from our sins by his blood,
and made us to be a kingdom,

priests serving his God and Father,
to him be glory and dominion
for ever and ever. Amen.

Look! He is coming with the clouds;
every eye will see him,
even those who pierced him;
and on his account all the tribes of the earth will
wail.

Glory to the Father, and to the Son,
and to the Holy Spirit:
as it was in the beginning, is now,
and will be for ever. Amen.

ANTIPHON "I AM THE ALPHA AND THE OMEGA,"
WHO IS AND WHO WAS AND WHO IS TO COME,
THE ALMIGHTY.

LITANY

For the one, holy, catholic, and apostolic Church
in all four quarters of the world, we pray:
~LORD, HAVE MERCY.

For the successors of Jude the apostle
and of all the holy apostles, we pray:
~LORD, HAVE MERCY.

For the faith once for all entrusted to the saints,
we pray:
~LORD, HAVE MERCY.

For the spiritual and temporal welfare of all
faithful Christians, we pray:

~Lord, have mercy.

For our urgent needs in time of great difficulty,
we pray:

~Lord, have mercy.

(Pause for prayers of intercession.)

By the prayers of the great Mother of God, Mary
most holy, of St. Jude the apostle, and of all the
saints, we pray:

~Lord, have mercy.

Prayer

Gracious God,
by the testimony of the holy apostles
you make us confident Christians,
relying on the good news of Jesus Christ.
By the prayers of Jude the apostle
may your Church grow continually
in the true faith and in good deeds.
We ask this through Christ our Lord.
~Amen.

To the only God our Savior, through Jesus Christ,
be glory, majesty, power, and authority,
now and for ever.
~Amen.

A Novena to
Mother Teresa of Calcutta

Mother Teresa is one of the most venerated people of the twentieth century. Born in Albania in 1910, she went to India as a nun-teacher but left her first vocation when she experienced the ultimate miseries of Calcutta. Armed with nothing but faith in God's providence, she devoted herself to alleviating the most afflicted of the poor: the street people and the dying. She offered them dignity, solace, and personal care when all others had abandoned them. When other women—and later men—came to her assistance, she formed two new religious congregations, the Missionaries of Charity, now serving the wretched of the earth in cities around the world. Her loving dedication drew worldwide applause and made her a counterbalance to the horrors of her century. Mother Teresa died in 1997 and was beatified by Pope John Paul II on October 19, 2003.

Who Is Jesus to Me?

The Word made flesh. The Bread of Life. The Victim offered for our sins on the cross. The Sacrifice offered at the holy mass for the sins of the world and mine. . . .

The Leper—to wash his wounds.
The Beggar—to give him a smile.
The Drunkard—to listen to him.
The Mental—to protect him.
The Little One—to embrace him.
The Blind—to lead him.

The Dumb—to speak for him.
The Crippled—to walk with him.
The Drug Addict—to befriend him.
The Prostitute—to remove from danger
and befriend her.
The Prisoner—to be visited.
The Old—to be served.[69]

In the name of the Father, ✝ and of the Son,
and of the Holy Spirit.
~Amen.

Children shall be yours in place of your forebears.
~May the peoples praise you from age to
age.

Hymn

Let us with joy our voices raise
In that heroic woman's praise,
Whose courage, strength and holy fame
Have given her an honored name.

O strength of all the strong, God's Son,
Through whom alone great deeds are done,
By your great strength and holy prayer
May we bear witness ev'rywhere.

Praise God the Father and the Son
And Holy Spirit, Three in One,
Who gave this noble woman grace
A life of virtue to embrace.[70]

PSALM 127   GOD'S GOODNESS

ANTIPHON Children ARE A HERITAGE FROM THE
    LORD.

Unless the Lord builds the house,
those who build it labor in vain.
Unless the Lord guards the city,
the guard keeps watch in vain.

It is vain that you rise up early
and go late to rest,
eating the bread of distressing work;
for God gives sleep to the beloved of the Lord.

Children are indeed a heritage from the Lord,
the fruit of the womb is a reward.
Like arrows in the hand of a warrior
are the children of one's youth.

Happy are those who have
a quiver full of them!
They shall not be put to shame
when they speak with their enemies in the gate.

ANTIPHON CHILDREN ARE A HERITAGE FROM THE
    LORD.

PSALM PRAYER

Let us pray *(pause for quiet prayer)*:

God of infinite goodness,
Mother Teresa knew the great truths
of working with you and for you
in the most abandoned of your creatures.

May you enrich the Church
with a worldwide family of disciples
to share her charitable designs
and to glorify the gospel of your Son,
who lives and reigns with you and the Holy Spirit,
now and for ever.
~Amen.

READING   THE SHEMA   DEUTERONOMY 6:4–7

Hear, O Israel: The Lord is our God, the Lord
alone. You shall love the Lord your God with
all your heart, and with all your soul, and with
all your might. Keep these words that I am
commanding you today in your heart. Recite them
to your children and talk about them when you
are at home and when you are away, when you lie
down and when you rise.

SILENCE

RESPONSE

The second commandment is like the first:
~You shall love your neighbor as yourself.

CANTICLE OF HANNAH   I SAMUEL 2:1a–4, 7–8[71]

ANTIPHON I give you a new commandment,
THAT YOU LOVE ONE ANOTHER,
JUST AS I HAVE LOVED YOU, ALLELUIA!

My heart exults in the Lord;
my strength is exalted in my God.
There is no Holy One like the Lord,

no one besides you;
there is no Rock like our God.

For the LORD is a God of knowledge;
and by your actions you are weighed.
The bows of the mighty are broken,
but the feeble gird on strength.

You, LORD, make poor and make rich;
you bring low and you also exalt.
You raise up the poor from the dust;
and lift the needy from the ash heap.

You make them sit with princes
and inherit a seat of honor.
For yours, O LORD, are the pillars of the earth,
and on them you have set the world.

To the Ruler of the ages, immortal, invisible,
the only wise God,
be honor and glory, through Jesus Christ,
for ever and ever. Amen.

ANTIPHON I GIVE YOU A NEW COMMANDMENT,
THAT YOU LOVE ONE ANOTHER,
JUST AS I HAVE LOVED YOU, ALLELUIA!

LITANY
We thank you for the life and charity
        of Mother Teresa of Calcutta:
~WE THANK YOU, LORD.

We thank you for the infinite condescension
        of the eternal Word of God made flesh:
~WE THANK YOU, LORD.

We thank you for the gift of the two great
    commandments of our holy religion:
~We thank you, Lord.

We thank you for the challenging Beatitudes of
    the Sermon on the Mount:
~We thank you, Lord.

We thank you for holy and loving lives of those
    who serve the sick and dying:
~We thank you, Lord.

We thank you for those who bury the dead and
    pray for their eternal rest:
~We thank you, Lord.

We thank you for the two religious families
    founded by Mother Teresa:
~We thank you, Lord.

(Here we state our needs.)

We thank you for the prayers of Our Lady of
    Mercy, of Mother Teresa of Calcutta, and
    of all the saints in glory:
~We thank you, Lord.

PRAYER
Holy and deathless One,
in both covenants women sang your praise
and glorified your divine providence.
Grateful for the life and teaching
of Mother Teresa of Calcutta,

we ask you to inspire us by the great
   commandments
of love of God and love of neighbor
that you taught us through Moses the prophet
and through your own dear Son, our Savior,
who lives and reigns with you and the Holy Spirit,
now and for ever.
   ~Amen.

May the Lord ✝ bless us and take care of us.
   ~Amen.
May the Lord be kind and gracious to us.
   ~Amen.
May the Lord look on us with favor
   and give us peace. ~Amen.

A Novena to Good Pope John XXIII

Angelo Roncalli (1881–1963) was a priest of great simplicity, friendliness, and quiet goodness who worked for
many years as a papal diplomat among the Orthodox
churches of Eastern Europe. In 1944 he was appointed
papal nuncio to Paris to help settle the pressing difficulties of the Church of France (which he did with
great finesse) and was subsequently made Patriarch of
Venice in 1953. At the death of Pope Pius XII in 1958,
he was unexpectedly elected to the See of Peter and
proved to be a most delightful, lovable, and audacious
pope for four and a half momentous years. In 1962 he
called and presided over the first session of the Second
Vatican Council, where he suggested a program
of renewal and rejuvenation for the Roman Church
that would fit it for the task of reunion with the other

churches of Christ. Good Pope John was beatified by Pope John Paul II in 2000. His tomb in St. Peter's Basilica coruscates with miracles.

Light shines forth for the just
~And joy for the upright of heart.

Rejoice, you just, in the Lord;
~Give glory to God's holy name.

Hymn
I bind unto myself today
The strong name of the Trinity,
By invocation of the same,
The Three in One, and One in Three.

I bind this day to me for ever,
By power of faith, Christ's incarnation;
His baptism in the Jordan river;
His death on the cross for my salvation;
His bursting from the spiced tomb;
His riding up the heavenly way;
His coming at the day of doom;
I bind unto myself today.[72]

Psalm 98   The Lord Does Marvelous Things
Antiphon Break forth in joyous song to the Lord.

O sing to the Lord a new song,
for the Lord has done marvelous things.
God's right hand and holy arm
have gotten the victory.

The Lord has declared victory,
and has revealed vindication
in the sight of the nations.

The Lord has remembered steadfast love
and faithfulness to the house of Israel.
All the ends of the earth have seen
the victory of our God.

Make a joyful noise to the Lord, all the earth;
break forth into joyous song and sing praises!
Sing praises to the Lord with the lyre,
with the lyre and the sound of melody!
With trumpets and the sound of the horn
make a joyful noise before the Ruler, the Lord!

Let the sea roar and all that fills it;
the world and those who dwell in it!
Let the floods clap their hands;
let the hills sing for joy together before the Lord,
who comes to judge the earth.
The Lord will judge the world with righteousness,
and the peoples with equity.

ANTIPHON BREAK FORTH IN JOYOUS SONG TO THE
LORD.

PSALM PRAYER
Let us pray *(pause for quiet prayer):*

Good Shepherd of the flock,
be mindful of your holy Church
in all four quarters of the earth.

Increase its holiness
and its zeal for the conversion
of the whole human race
so that they all may break forth in joyous song
to the Lord and Savior of the world,
who lives and reigns with you and the Holy Spirit,
now and for ever.
~Amen.

READING   TEND GOD'S FLOCK   1 PETER 5:1–4
Now as an elder myself and a witness of the
sufferings of Christ, as well as one who shares in
the glory to be revealed, I exhort the elders among
you to tend the flock of God that is in your charge,
exercising the oversight, not under compulsion but
willingly, as God would have you do it—not for
sordid gain but eagerly. Do not lord it over those
in your charge, but be examples to the flock. And
when the chief shepherd appears, you will win the
crown of glory that never fades away.

SILENCE

RESPONSE
If any of you suffers as a Christian,
~GLORIFY GOD BECAUSE YOU BEAR THIS NAME.

CANTICLE OF ZACHARY   LUKE 1:68–79[73]
ANTIPHON His name is John AND HE WILL BE
    CALLED THE PROPHET OF THE MOST HIGH,
    ALLELUIA!

Blessed are you, † Lord, the God of Israel,

you have come to your people and set them free.
You have raised up for us a mighty Savior,
born of the house of your servant David.

Through your holy prophets, you promised of old
    to save us from our enemies,
    from the hands of all who hate us,
    to show mercy to our forebears,
    and to remember your holy covenant.

This was the oath you swore to our father
    Abraham:
    to set us free from the hands of our enemies,
    free to worship you without fear,
    holy and righteous before you,
    all the days of our life.

And you, my child, shall be called the prophet of
    the Most High,
for you will go before the Lord to prepare the way,
to give God's people knowledge of salvation
by the forgiveness of their sins.

In the tender compassion of our God
the dawn from on high shall break upon us,
to shine on those who dwell in darkness
    and the shadow of death,
and to guide our feet into the way of peace.

Glory to the Holy and Undivided Trinity:
now and always and for ever and ever. Amen.

ANTIPHON His name is John and he will be called the prophet of the Most High, alleluia!

LITANY OF THE PRECIOUS BLOOD
(SEE PAGES 248–251)

NOVENA PRAYER
Good Pope John,
kind and zealous shepherd of the flock of Christ,
please be our intercessor before the throne of grace
as we set our needs before you.
(Here we state our needs.)
As you have won the crown of glory that never
      fades,
hear us and help us, we humbly pray,
by the merits of Jesus Christ, our blessed Lord.
~Amen.

May the Word made flesh, full of grace and truth,
✝ bless us and keep us.
~Amen.

A Novena to Dorothy Day

Dorothy Day (1897–1980), cofounder with Peter Maurin of the Catholic Worker movement, is more of an inspiration for her fellow Catholics than anyone in American history. By her dedication to the gospel, to the daily liturgy, to the poor, to peacemaking, and to the renewal of a society that would make it easier to be Christian, she drew hearts and minds to a fuller and deeper commitment to Christ and his Church. She stood for a challenging form of Christianity that confronted us with the severe demands of the gospel without compromise and made the Sermon on the Mount understandable and practical for laypeople and priests alike. By her lived experience, her ceaseless travels, and her fervor, she raised up a whole generation of "new" Catholics who will never forget her or her ideals.

Blessed be ✝ the Holy and Undivided Trinity,
~NOW AND ALWAYS AND FOR EVER AND EVER.

HYMN

Christ be with me, Christ within me,
Christ behind me, Christ before me,
Christ beside me, Christ to win me,
Christ to comfort and restore me.

Christ beneath me, Christ above me,
Christ in quiet, Christ in danger,
Christ in hearts of all that love me,
Christ in mouth of friend and stranger.[74]

PSALM 113   SERVANTS AND FRIENDS OF GOD

ANTIPHON Blessed be the poor in spirit
FOR THEIRS IS THE KINGDOM OF HEAVEN.

Praise, O servants of the Lord,
praise the name of the Lord!
Blessed be the name of the Lord
from this time forth and for evermore!
From the rising of the sun to its setting
the name of the Lord is to be praised.

The Lord is high above all nations,
God's glory above the heavens!
Who is like the Lord our God,
who is seated on high,
who looks far down
upon the heavens and the earth?

God raises the poor from the dust,
and lifts the needy from the ash heap,
to make them sit with nobles,
with the nobles of God's people.

God gives the barren woman a home,
making her the joyous mother of children.

ANTIPHON BLESSED BE THE POOR IN SPIRIT,
FOR THEIRS IS THE KINGDOM OF HEAVEN.

PSALM PRAYER

Let us pray *(pause for quiet prayer):*

God of mercy and compassion,
with Dorothy Day we praise you unceasingly
from the rising of the sun to its setting.
By her devotion to intercessory prayer,
raise up new disciples of the gospel of peace
who will do your will in the world.
We ask this through Christ our Lord.
~AMEN.

Brothers and sisters, since we are surrounded by
so great a cloud of witnesses, let us also lay aside
every weight and the sin that clings so closely,
and let us run with perseverance the race that
is set before us, looking to Jesus the pioneer and
perfecter of our faith, who for the sake of the
joy that was set before him endured the cross,
disregarding its shame, and has taken his seat at
the right hand of the throne of God.

SILENCE

RESPONSE

In your struggle against sin
~YOU HAVE NOT YET RESISTED TO THE POINT OF
SHEDDING YOUR BLOOD.

SONG OF THE CHURCH *TE DEUM LAUDAMUS*[75]

We praise you, O God,
we acclaim you as Lord;
all creation worships you,
the Father everlasting.

To you all angels, all the powers of heaven,
the cherubim and seraphim, sing in endless praise:
Holy, holy, holy Lord, God of power and might,
heaven and earth are full of your glory.

The glorious company of apostles praise you.
The noble fellowship of prophets praise you.
The white-robed army of martyrs praise you.

Throughout the world the holy Church acclaims you:
  Father, of majesty unbounded,
  your true and only Son, worthy of all praise,
  the Holy Spirit, advocate and guide.

You, Christ, are the king of glory,
the eternal Son of the Father.
When you took our flesh to set us free
you humbly chose the Virgin's womb.

You overcame the sting of death
and opened the kingdom of heaven to all believers.
You are seated at God's right hand in glory.
We believe that you will come to be our judge.

Come then, Lord, and help your people,
bought with the price of your own blood,
and bring us with your saints
to glory everlasting.

LITANY

With Dorothy Day of New York, let us pray to the
  Lord.
~LORD, HAVE MERCY. CHRIST, HAVE MERCY.
  LORD, HAVE MERCY.

By her delight in assisting at daily Mass, let us
  pray to the Lord.
~LORD, HAVE MERCY. CHRIST, HAVE MERCY.
  LORD, HAVE MERCY.

By her fervent love of the Psalms and the Liturgy
  of the Hours, let us pray to the Lord.

~Lord, have mercy. Christ, have mercy.
Lord, have mercy.

By her profound understanding of the saints who were devoted to the poor and abandoned, let us pray to the Lord.
~Lord, have mercy. Christ, have mercy.
Lord, have mercy.

By her personal poverty and self-denial, let us pray to the Lord.
~Lord, have mercy. Christ, have mercy.
Lord, have mercy.

By her passionate devotion to Christ crucified, let us pray to the Lord.
~Lord, have mercy. Christ, have mercy.
Lord, have mercy.

By her fervent dedication to social justice, let us pray to the Lord.
~Lord, have mercy. Christ, have mercy.
Lord, have mercy.

(Pause for intercessory prayer.)

By her love of the Great Mother of God, Mary most holy, of St. Thérèse of Lisieux, and of all the saints, let us pray to the Lord.
~Lord, have mercy. Christ, have mercy.
Lord, have mercy.

NOVENA PRAYER

Lord Jesus Christ,
in the shadow of two world wars
and the age of the atom bomb,
you raised up Dorothy Day to inspire us
with a fresh understanding of the Sermon on the
    Mount
and the reconciling Christ who preached it to us.
May her prayers accompany us on our journey
to the land of peace and plenty
where you bring us all together
under the shadow of your cross
that heals all our wounds.
Blessed be your holy name, now and for ever.
~AMEN.

May the Word made flesh, the Son of Mary,
✝ bless us and keep us, now and for ever.
~AMEN.

A Novena to the Jesuit Martyrs of North America

The first martyrs in North America were a group of seventeenth-century Jesuit missionaries preaching the gospel among the Huron Indians of southwestern Ontario and the Iroquois of upper New York State. Their astonishing faith, courage, and perseverance in the midst of unbelievable conditions and the cruelest of tortures mark them down as genuine Christian heroes.

Their close alliance, however, with the government of New France and with the fur trade seems to have somewhat compromised their religious mission and brought on the almost total destruction of the Huron people whose, souls they desired so ardently to save.

Fathers Jean de Brébeuf, Gabriel Lallemant, Charles Garnier, Noel Chabanel, and Antoine Daniel were martyred in Ontario, Canada (1648–1649). Father Isaac Jogues and the lay oblates René Goupil and Jean de la Lande were done to death in what is now upper New York State (1642–1646). These martyrs are the secondary patrons of Canada. Their feast day is September 26 in Canada; it is October 19 in the United States.

In the name of the Father, ✝ and of the Son, and of the Holy Spirit.
~Amen.

Precious in the eyes of the Lord
~Is the death of the faithful.

Hymn
The martyrs, living now with Christ,
In suffering were tried,
Their anguish overthrown by love,
When on his cross they died.

Across the centuries they come,
In constancy unmoved,
Their loving hearts make no complaint;
In silence they are proved.

For who has ever measured love
Or weighed it in the hand?

Yet God, who knows the inmost heart,
Gives them the promised land.

Praise Father, Son and Spirit blest,
Who guide us through the night,
In ways that reach beyond the stars
To everlasting light.[76]

PSALM 18:1–6, 16–17   SECURITY IN GOD ALONE

ANTIPHON Blessed are you who weep now,
FOR YOU WILL LAUGH.

I love you, O Lord, my strength.
The Lord is my rock, my fortress, my deliverer,
my God, my rock in whom I take refuge,
my shield and the horn of my salvation, my
    stronghold.
I call upon the Lord who is worthy to be praised,
and I shall be saved from my enemies.

The cords of death encompassed me,
the torrents of perdition assailed me;
the cords of Sheol entangled me,
the snares of death confronted me.

In my distress I called upon the Lord;
to my God I cried for help.
From the temple the Lord heard my voice,
and my cry reached God's ears.

The Lord reached down from on high and took me,
drew me out of mighty waters,
delivered me from my strong enemy,

from those who hated me;
for they were too strong for me.

ANTIPHON BLESSED ARE YOU WHO WEEP NOW,
FOR YOU WILL LAUGH.

PSALM PRAYER

Let us pray *(pause for quiet prayer)*:

Just God,
whose throne is in heaven,
you do indeed love justice
and hate the wrongs
that destroy the upright by stealth and violence.
Look down on the peoples of the earth
and bring order and peace
out of chaos and injustice.
In Jesus' name, we ask it.
~AMEN.

READING   TAKE UP THE CROSS   MARK 8:34–38

Jesus called the crowd with his disciples, and said to them, "If any want to become my followers, let them deny themselves and take up their cross and follow me. For those who want to save their life will lose it, and those who lose their life for my sake, and for the sake of the gospel, will save it. For what will it profit them to gain the whole world and forfeit their life? Indeed, what can they give in return for their life? Those who are ashamed of me and of my words in this adulterous and sinful generation, of them the Son of Man

will also be ashamed when he comes in the glory
of his Father with the holy angels."

SILENCE

RESPONSE

God will wipe away every tear from their eyes,
    alleluia!

~DEATH WILL BE NO MORE, ALLELUIA!

CANTICLE OF OUR EXALTED LORD　　PHILIPPIANS 2:6–11

ANTIPHON　May I never boast of anything EXCEPT
    THE CROSS OF OUR LORD JESUS CHRIST,
    ALLELUIA!
BY WHICH THE WORLD HAS BEEN CRUCIFIED TO ME,
AND I TO THE WORLD, ALLELUIA!

Though he was in the form of God,
Christ Jesus did not regard equality with God
as something to be exploited,
but emptied himself,
taking the form of a slave,
being born in human likeness.

And being found in human form,
he humbled himself
and became obedient to the point of death—
even death on a cross.

Therefore God also highly exalted him
and gave him the name
that is above every name,
so that at the name of Jesus

every knee should bend,
in heaven and on earth and under the earth,
and every tongue should confess
that Jesus Christ is Lord,
to the glory of God the Father.

ANTIPHON MAY I NEVER BOAST OF ANYTHING
   EXCEPT THE CROSS OF OUR LORD JESUS
   CHRIST, ALLELUIA!
BY WHICH THE WORLD HAS BEEN CRUCIFIED TO
   ME, AND I TO THE WORLD, ALLELUIA!

LITANY

Teacher of righteousness and King of martyrs:
~GRACE THE CHURCH WITH ZEAL AND PRUDENCE.

By the blood and relics of the first martyrs
   of North America:
~GRACE THE CHURCH WITH ZEAL AND PRUDENCE.

By their sacrifice of home, family, and friends:
~GRACE THE CHURCH WITH ZEAL AND PRUDENCE.

By their lack of respect for mere human reason:
~GRACE THE CHURCH WITH ZEAL AND PRUDENCE.

By their fervent devotion to the truth as they saw it:
~GRACE THE CHURCH WITH ZEAL AND PRUDENCE.

By their willingness to lay down their lives for
   their friends and converts:
~GRACE THE CHURCH WITH ZEAL AND PRUDENCE.

By their total commitment to the gospel of peace:
~GRACE THE CHURCH WITH ZEAL AND PRUDENCE.

(Pause for intercessory prayer.)

By the prayers of Mary, Queen of martyrs, of the
    Jesuit martyrs of North America, and of all the
    martyr band:

~GRACE THE CHURCH WITH ZEAL AND PRUDENCE.

PRAYER

God of justice and peace,
hallow the Americas by the heroic mission
and total sacrifice of the Jesuit martyrs,
John de Brébeuf, Isaac Jogues,
and their faithful companions.
By the success and failure of their lives
teach your Church both zeal and a new prudence
in converting the native peoples of the world.
We ask this through Christ Jesus our Lord.
~AMEN.

May the God of peace sanctify us entirely
and † keep us sound and blameless
at the coming of our Lord Jesus Christ.
~AMEN.

A Novena to
Oscar Arnulfo Romero—
Archbishop, Patriot, and Martyr

As he grew in office, Archbishop Romero learned the
price to be paid for becoming "the voice for the voice-
less" and for preaching the Good News in the face of
the mighty. On March 24, 1980, an assassin shot him

down as he was offering evening Mass in the Carmelite cancer hospital in San Salvador, El Salvador. He died for justice for the poor and helpless and was at once accepted by the people as a martyr and a saint. His funeral was attended by some 150,000 of his people and by bishops and dignitaries from many countries in Latin America and Europe. His tomb in the Metropolitan Cathedral of San Salvador is the destination of pilgrims throughout Central America. Hundreds of cures are attributed to his intercession.

Oscar Romero

The dead are not dead—that we can learn from Oscar Romero. He is more alive than ever. It was impossible to kill him. . . .

He even organizes us, which is to say, he converts us. He draws us into the great process of conversion, which today goes from the poor to the rich, from the uneducated to college graduates. In the same way that he was converted mainly through the death of his friend, the Jesuit Father Rutilio Grande, so too his death converts us and many others who for a long time did not want to recognize reality. The dead are not dead—neither Romero nor the 60,000 others who had to lay down their lives in the so-called "low intensity" war in El Salvador. They are not forgotten even among us. We are not alone, nor cut off from the root which sustains us.

We have with one another a tradition that sustains us. We can remember others who believed and hoped before us. Many of them were tortured and murdered, but that did not destroy the cause of justice, because it is the cause of God, which is to say the cause of the poor.

What I am trying to say has been said for a long time and more clearly by the people of El Salvador. They long since canonized Bishop Oscar Arnulfo Romero. Some day the Vatican in Rome will take note and follow suit. But in this case the people have taken the lead and they call him a saint, a comforter, a helper.[77]

In the name of the Father, **✝** and of the Son, and of the Holy Spirit.
~AMEN.

Nothing can separate us from the love of God
~THAT COMES TO US IN CHRIST JESUS OUR LORD.

HYMN

King of the martyrs' noble band,
Crown of the true in every land,
Strength of the pilgrims on their way
Beacon by night and cloud by day.

Hear us now as we celebrate
Faith undeterred by ruthless hate;
Hear and forgive us, for we too
Know very well the wrong we do.

Dying, through you they overcame;
Living, were faithful to your name.
Turn our rebellious hearts, and thus
Win a like victory in us.

Glory to God the Father be,
Glory to Christ who set us free;
And to the Spirit, living flame,
Glory unceasing we proclaim.[78]

PSALM 11   SECURITY IN GOD

ANTIPHON The Lord HATES THE LOVER OF
   VIOLENCE.

In the Lord I take refuge.
How can you say to me,
"Flee like a bird to the mountains;

See how the wicked bend the bow,
they have fitted the arrow to the string,
to shoot in the dark at the upright of heart.
If the foundations are destroyed,
what can the righteous do?"

The Lord whose throne is in heaven,
sees and examines all mortals.
The Lord tests the righteous and the wicked,
and hates the lover of violence.

The Lord is righteous
and loves righteous deeds;
the upright shall behold the face of the Lord.

ANTIPHON THE LORD HATES THE LOVER OF
   VIOLENCE.

PSALM PRAYER

Let us pray *(pause for quiet prayer)*:

God of justice and mercy,

you provide your Church
with fresh witnesses in every age.
By the prayer of the holy martyrs,
may we meet the challenges of the gospel
at all times and in all places.
In Jesus' name we ask it.
~AMEN.

READING
THE DEATH OF JESUS
2 CORINTHIANS 4:8–11

We are afflicted in every way, but not crushed;
perplexed, but not driven to despair; persecuted,
but not forsaken; struck down, but not destroyed;
always carrying in the body the death of Jesus, so
that the life of Jesus may also be made visible in
our bodies. For while we live, we are always being
given up to death for Jesus' sake, so that the life of
Jesus may be made visible in our mortal flesh.

SILENCE

RESPONSE
If we are being afflicted, alleluia!
~IT IS FOR YOUR CONSOLATION AND SALVATION,
ALLELUIA!

CANTICLE OF SIMEON
LUKE 2:29–32[79]

ANTIPHON We know THAT THE ONE WHO RAISED
THE LORD JESUS WILL RAISE US ALSO WITH
JESUS, ALLELUIA!

Now, Lord, let your servant go in peace:
your word has been fulfilled.

My own eyes have seen the salvation
which you have prepared in the sight of every
    people:

a light to reveal you to the nations
and the glory of your people Israel.

Glory to the Father, and to the Son,
and to the Holy Spirit:
as it was in the beginning, is now,
and will be for ever. Amen.

ANTIPHON WE KNOW THAT THE ONE WHO RAISED
THE LORD JESUS WILL RAISE US ALSO WITH
JESUS, ALLELUIA!

LITANY

Lord Jesus, King of martyrs:
~BE OUR LIFE AND OUR SALVATION.

By Archbishop Romero's commitment to social
    justice:
~BE OUR LIFE AND OUR SALVATION.

By his fearless and outspoken championing of
    peace:
~BE OUR LIFE AND OUR SALVATION.

By his refusal to serve the idols of war and death:
~BE OUR LIFE AND OUR SALVATION.

By the fear and loneliness of his final days:
~BE OUR LIFE AND OUR SALVATION.

By his blood spilled on the altar table of his Savior:
~BE OUR LIFE AND OUR SALVATION.

By his precious death for the Church of the
   oppressed:
~Be our life and our salvation.

(Pause for intercessory prayer.)

By the prayers of Mary, Queen of martyrs, of your
   martyr bishop, Oscar Romero, and of all the
   white-robed martyrs:
~Be our life and our salvation.

Prayer

By the example and prayers
of your martyred archbishop,
Oscar Romero of San Salvador,
give us the courage, O God,
to stand for justice in the face
of wickedness in high places
and to embrace the poor and humble
who are the special images of Christ in the world.
We ask this in Jesus' name.
~Amen.

By the witness and blood of the holy martyrs,
✝ may we drink of the cup of salvation.
~Amen.

A Triduum to a Patron Saint

When we are baptized, we take the name of a particular saint who then becomes our patron for the rest of our life. We pray to this saint for divine guidance and protection, and we honor him or her in some way on the appropriate feast/baptismal day or at any other time.

In the name of the Father, ✝ and of the Son,
and of the Holy Spirit.
~AMEN.

Be strong, and let your heart take courage,
~ALL YOU WHO WAIT FOR THE LORD.

HYMN
Fight the good fight with all your might,
Christ is your strength and Christ your right;
Lay hold on life, and it shall be
Your joy and crown eternally.

Run the straight race through God's good grace,
Lift up your eyes and see God's face;
Life with its path before you lies,
Christ is the path and Christ the prize.

Cast care aside; upon your guide
Lean, and God's mercy will provide;
Lean, and the trusting soul shall prove
Christ is its life, and Christ its love.[80]

PSALM 15   HOLINESS TO THE LORD
ANTIPHON Be holy AS I AM HOLY, SAYS THE LORD.

O Lord, who shall dwell in your tent?
Who shall dwell on your holy hill?

The one who walks blamelessly,
and does what is right,
and speaks truth from the heart;

who does not slander with the tongue.
and does no evil to a friend,
nor takes up a reproach with a neighbor;

in whose eyes a reproach is despised,
but who honors those who fear the Lord;
who does not loan money at interest,
and does not take a bribe against the innocent.

Whoever does these things shall never be moved.

ANTIPHON BE HOLY AS I AM HOLY, SAYS THE
LORD.

PSALM PRAYER
Let us pray *(pause for quiet prayer):*

Holy and deathless God,
you charge both saints and angels
to guard us in all our ways.
As we put our trust in you
and praise you in all the saints,
may their prayers come to our assistance.
We ask this through Christ our Lord.
~AMEN.

READING   A PROGRAM OF HOLINESS   MICAH 6:8
God has told you, O mortal, what is good; and
what does the LORD require of you but to do
justice, and to love kindness, and to walk humbly
with your God?

SILENCE

Guard me, O Lord, as the apple of your eye.
~Hide me in the shadow of your wings.

Canticle of Solomon **Wisdom 6:12–16**

Antiphon The righteous will live for ever,
and their reward is with the Lord.

Wisdom is radiant and unfading,
and she is easily discerned
    by those who love her,
and is found by those who seek her.

She hastens to make herself known
to those who desire her.
One who rises early to seek her
    will have no difficulty,
for she will be found sitting at the gate.

To fix one's thoughts on her is perfect
        understanding,
and one who is vigilant on her account
    will soon be free from care,
because she goes about seeking those worthy of her,
and she graciously appears to them in their paths,
and meets them in every thought.

Glory to the Father, and to the Son,
and to the Holy Spirit:
as it was in the beginning, is now,
and will be for ever. Amen.

Antiphon The righteous will live for ever,
and their reward is with the Lord.

LITANY OF THE BEATITUDES

Lord Jesus, teacher of righteousness;
~GIVE US TRUE HAPPINESS AND EVERY BLESSING.

Bless the poor and humble in spirit;
~MAKE THEM INHERIT THE KINGDOM OF HEAVEN.

Bless those who mourn for lost blessings;
~BE THEIR COMFORT IN TIME OF TROUBLE.

Bless those who are meek and humble of heart;
~LET THEM INHERIT WHAT GOD HAS PROMISED.

Bless those who hunger and thirst for what God
    requires;
~AND FILL THEM WITH DIVINE WHOLENESS.

Bless those who are merciful toward others;
~MAY GOD BE MERCIFUL TO THEM IN TURN.

Bless those who are pure in heart;
~LET THEM SEE GOD IN THE LIGHT OF GLORY.

Bless those who make peace on earth;
~AND CALL THEM THE CHILDREN OF GOD.

Bless those who are persecuted for being holy;
~GIVE THEM POSSESSION OF THE KINGDOM OF GOD.

Bless those who are slandered and insulted for
    your sake;
~MAKE THEM HAPPY AND GLAD
    FOR THEIR REWARD IS GREAT IN THEIR
    HEAVENLY HOME.

(Here we pray to our guardian angel and patron saint.)

God of all holiness,
you are glorified in all your saints
and in crowning their merits
you are but crowning your own gifts.
Surrounded by such a crowd of witnesses,
help us to run our appointed race
and with them receive the never-fading garland
     of glory.
We ask this through Jesus Christ our Lord.
~Amen.[81]

May the divine assistance ✝ remain always with us.
~Amen.

A Novena or Triduum
for a Pilgrimage

At God's prompting Abraham and Sarah went on a
pilgrimage seeking God and a Promised Land. Fleeing
from Egypt, Moses and the Israelites journeyed through
the wilderness of Sinai for forty years and finally
crossed the Jordan into the Promised Land, led by the
Tent of Promise containing the Ark of the Covenant
with the Tablets of the Law. With the establishment
of the temple came the obligation (obeyed by Jesus
himself) to attend the three great festivals in Jerusalem.
Jesus' death and resurrection occurred in the midst of
a great river of pilgrims who were present at Passover,
and Pentecost took place fifty days later at a similar pilgrimage swarming with Jews "from every nation under
heaven" (Acts 2:5).

Ever since the Peace of the Church in the early fourth century, pilgrims have been seeking the Holy Land to venerate the sacred spots where Jesus was born, preached the Gospel, suffered, died, and rose again, and where the primitive Church took its origins. Great shrine churches were erected at Bethlehem and Nazareth, on Golgotha, in Rome over the graves of Peter and Paul, and in Jerusalem at the tomb of Mary, where she was assumed into heaven. In the Middle Ages pilgrimage was even more in vogue: to the tombs of Peter and Paul in Rome, to the grave of St. Martin of Tours in Gaul, to the shrine of St. James of Compostela in northwest Spain, to the bejeweled shrine of St. Thomas of Canterbury in England. In modern times pilgrims in great numbers still flow to shrines all over the world. They go seeking rest and spiritual renewal, inspiration from the lives of the saints, and answers to their devout prayers for spiritual and temporal needs.

In the name of the Father, ✝ and of the Son, and of the Holt Spirit.

~Amen.

Hymn

Christ be near at either hand,
Christ behind, before me stand,
Christ with me where'er I go,
Christ around, above, below.

Christ be in my heart and mind,
Christ within my soul enshrined,
Christ control my wayward heart,
Christ abide and ne'er depart.

Christ my life and only way,
Christ my lantern night and day,
Christ be my unchanging friend,
Guide and guard me to the end.[82]

Psalm 122   A Pilgrim Song

Antiphon   Let us go to God's house.

I was glad when they said to me
"Let us go to the house of the Lord!"
Our feet are standing
within your gates, O Jerusalem!

Jerusalem is built as a city
bound tightly together,
to which the tribes go up,
the tribes of the Lord,
to give thanks to the name of the Lord,
as was decreed for Israel.

Thrones for judgment were set up there,
the thrones of the house of David.
Pray for the peace of Jerusalem:
"May they prosper who love you!
Peace be within your walls,
and security within your towers!"

For the sake of my relatives and friends,
I will say, "Peace be within you!"
For the sake of the house of the Lord our God,
I will seek your good.

Antiphon   Let us go to God's house.

PSALM PRAYER

Let us pray *(pause for quiet prayer):*

God of the city of peace,
as we go on pilgrimage
to the shrine of your presence,
fill us with longing for the peace
that passes all understanding.
Please grant this through Christ,
our blessed Lord and Savior.
~AMEN.

READING   THE HEAVENLY JERUSALEM   HEBREWS 12:22–24

You have come to Mount Zion and to the city of
the living God, the heavenly Jerusalem, and to
innumerable angels in festal gathering, and to
the assembly of the firstborn who are enrolled
in heaven, and to God the judge of all, and to
the spirits of the righteous made perfect, and to
Jesus, the mediator of a new covenant, and to the
sprinkled blood that speaks a better word than the
blood of Abel.

SILENCE

RESPONSE

Precious in the sight of the Lord
~IS THE DEATH OF THE FAITHFUL.

CANTICLE OF ISAIAH THE PROPHET (40:3–5, 9)

ANTIPHON My eyes have seen the salvation WHICH YOU HAVE PREPARED IN THE SIGHT OF EVERY PEOPLE.

A voice cries out:
"In the wilderness
prepare the way of the LORD,
make straight in the desert
a highway for our God.

Every valley shall be lifted up,
and every mountain and hill be made low;
the uneven ground shall become level,
and the rough places a plain.

Then the glory of the LORD shall be revealed,
and all people shall see it together,
for the mouth of the LORD has spoken."

Get you up to a high mountain, O Zion,
herald of good tidings;
lift up your voice with strength, O Jerusalem,
herald of good tidings,
lift it up, do not fear;
say to the cities of Judah,
"Here is your God!"

Glory to the Holy and Undivided Trinity:
now and always and for ever and ever. Amen.

ANTIPHON MY EYES HAVE SEEN THE SALVATION WHICH YOU HAVE PREPARED IN THE SIGHT OF EVERY PEOPLE.

An Appropriate Litany from pages 246–257

Lord's Prayer

Let us pray as Jesus taught us:
~Our Father in heaven . . . *(Continue in unison.)*

Prayer

Jesus, Messiah of Israel,
before your first coming
you sent prophets, priests, and kings
to prepare a way before you.
Stir up the preaching of the gospel in your Church
and turn our hearts to true repentance
that at your second coming to judge the world
we may be found an acceptable people in your
   sight;
for yours is the kingdom and the power and the
   glory,
now and for ever.
~Amen.

May the God of hope **†** fill us
with all joy and peace in believing,
so that we may abound in hope
by the power of the Holy Spirit.
~Amen.

Novenas for Special Occasions

A Novena in Time of Difficulties

Jesus exhorts us to bear life's difficulties and temptations and to unite them to his cross. Some events are so troublesome that we need the full assurance that God and the Church are still with us and support us in our hour of need. This novena is designed primarily for private prayer but could be used by a sympathetic group of friends of the afflicted person or family.

In the name of the Holy and Undivided Trinity, Father, ✝ Son, and Holy Spirit.
~Amen.

Lord, hear our prayer,
~And let our cry come unto you.

Hymn

All you who seek a comfort sure
In trouble and distress,
Whatever sorrows vex the mind
Or guilt the soul oppress,

Jesus who gave himself for you

Upon the cross to die,
Opens to you his sacred heart;
O, to that heart draw nigh.

You hear how kindly he invites,
You hear his words so blest:
"All you that labor come to me,
And I will give you rest."

Christ Jesus, joy of saints on high,
The hope of sinners here,
Attracted by those loving words
To you we lift our prayer.

Lord, wash our wounds in that dear blood
Which from your heart did flow;
New grace, new hope inspire, a new
And better heart bestow.[83]

PSALM 62:1–2, 5–8   GOD IS OUR ROCK

ANTIPHON God alone IS MY ROCK AND MY
SALVATION.

In silence I wait for God alone,
from whom my salvation comes.
God alone is my rock and my salvation,
my fortress; I shall never be shaken.

In silence I wait for God alone,
for my hope is from God,
who alone is my rock and my salvation,
my fortress; I shall not be shaken.

On God rests my deliverance and my honor;
my mighty rock, my refuge is God.

Trust in God at all times, O people;
pour out your heart before God
who is our refuge.

ANTIPHON GOD ALONE IS MY ROCK AND MY
SALVATION.

PSALM PRAYER
Let us pray *(pause for quiet prayer):*

Loving Father,
we pour out our hearts before you,
knowing that you are always on our side,
comforting, consoling, and strengthening.
Be our refuge in time of trouble
for you are our rock, our stronghold and our
fortress.
Be with us in Christ Jesus, our blessed Savior.
~AMEN.

	DIVINE	**MATTHEW**
READING	**PROVIDENCE**	**10:28–31**

Do not fear those who kill the body but cannot
kill the soul; rather fear him who can destroy
both soul and body in hell. Are not two sparrows
sold for a penny? Yet not one of them will fall to
the ground apart from your Father. And even the
hairs of your head are all counted. So do not be
afraid; you are of more value than many sparrows.

SILENCE

RESPONSE

Whoever does not take up the cross and follow me
~IS NOT WORTHY OF ME.

CANTICLE OF   EPHESIANS
ST. PAUL THE APOSTLE   2:4–7; 3:20–21

ANTIPHON Holy is God, ✝ HOLY AND STRONG,
HOLY AND LIVING FOR EVER.

You, O God, are rich in mercy,
out of your great love with which you loved us,
even when we were dead through our trespasses,
you made us alive together with Christ.

You raised us up with him
and seated us with him
in the heavenly places in Christ Jesus,
so that in the ages to come
you might show the immeasurable riches of your
    grace
in kindness toward us in Christ Jesus.

By your power at work within us
you are able to accomplish abundantly
far more than all we can ask or imagine.
To you be glory in the Church and in Christ Jesus
through all generations, for ever and ever. Amen.

ANTIPHON Holy is God, ✝ HOLY AND STRONG,
HOLY AND LIVING FOR EVER.

LITANY OF THE BEATITUDES

Lord Jesus, teacher of righteousness;
~GIVE US TRUE HAPPINESS AND EVERY BLESSING.

Bless the poor and humble in spirit;
~Make them inherit the kingdom of
   heaven.

Bless those who mourn for lost blessings;
~Be their comfort in time of trouble.

Bless those who are meek and humble of heart;
~Let them inherit what God has promised.

Bless those who hunger and thirst for what God
   requires;
~And fill them with divine wholeness.

Bless those who are merciful toward others;
~May God be merciful to them in turn.

Bless those who are pure in heart;
~Let them see God in the light of glory.

Bless those who make peace on earth;
~And call them the children of God.

Bless those who are persecuted for being holy;
~Give them possession of the kingdom of
   God.

Bless those who are slandered and insulted for
   your sake;
~Make them happy and glad for their
   reward is great in their heavenly home.

Novena Prayer
Compassionate and merciful God,
by grace you live in our inmost being

and stand by us in every difficulty.
Be with us in our hour of need.
(Here we state our needs.)
By the prayers of the great Mother of God
and of the whole company of heaven,
calm our troubled hearts,
and have us put our trust in you.
We ask this through Christ our Lord.
~AMEN.

May the Lord ✝ direct our hearts in the love of God
and the patience of Christ.
~AMEN.

A Novena or Triduum
of Thanksgiving

In time of need we often have recourse to a novena of intercession, but sometimes we forget to thank God—whatever the answer—at its conclusion. Paul the apostle teaches us the right order: "Do not worry about anything, but in everything by prayer and supplication *with thanksgiving* let your requests be made known to God" (Philippians 4:6); and "I urge that supplications, prayers, intercessions, and *thanksgivings* be made for everyone" (1 Timothy 2:1).

In the name of the Father, ✝ and of the Son,
and of the Holy Spirit.
~AMEN.

HYMN

Now thank we all our God
With hearts and hands and voices,
Who wondrous things has done,
In whom this world rejoices;
Who from our mothers' arms,
Has blessed us on our way
With countless gifts of love,
And still is ours today.

O may this gracious God
Through all our life be near us,
With ever joyful hearts
And blessed peace to cheer us;
Preserve us in his grace,
And guide us in distress,
And free us from all sin,
Till heaven we possess.

All praise and thanks to God
The Father now be given,
The Son and Spirit blest,
Who reigns in highest heaven,
Eternal, Triune God,
Whom earth and heav'n adore;
For thus it was, is now,
And shall be evermore.[84]

PSALM 116:10–19   GRATITUDE

ANTIPHON Give thanks to the Lord who is good,
FOR GOD'S LOVE ENDURES FOR EVER.

I kept my faith, even when I said,
"I am greatly afflicted."
I said in my consternation,
"All humans are a vain hope."

What shall I return to the Lord
for all God's gifts to me?
I will lift up the cup of salvation
and call on the name of the Lord.

I will pay my vows to the Lord
in the presence of all God's people.
Precious in the sight of the Lord
is the death of the faithful.

O Lord, I am your servant;
I am your servant, the child of your handmaid.
You have loosed my bonds.
I will offer to you the sacrifice of thanksgiving
and call on the name of the Lord.

I will pay my vows to the Lord,
in the presence of all God's people,
in the courts of the house of the Lord,
in your midst, O Jerusalem.

ANTIPHON GIVE THANKS TO THE LORD WHO IS
GOOD, FOR GOD'S LOVE ENDURES FOR EVER.

PSALM PRAYER

Let us pray *(pause for quiet prayer):*

Gracious God,
you are goodness itself

and you care for us unceasingly.
As we call upon your holy name,
please accept our sacrifice of thanksgiving
in and through Christ Jesus,
our blest and only Savior.
~AMEN.

FAITH AND
READING   **WHOLENESS**   **LUKE 17:12–19**

As Jesus entered a village, ten lepers approached
him. Keeping their distance, they called out,
saying, "Jesus, Master, have mercy on us!" When
he saw them, he said to them, "Go and show
yourselves to the priests." And as they went, they
were made clean. Then one of them, when he saw
that he was healed, turned back, praising God
with a loud voice. He prostrated himself at Jesus'
feet and thanked him. And he was a Samaritan.
Then Jesus asked, "Were not ten made clean? But
the other nine, where are they? Was none of them
found to return and give praise to God except this
foreigner?" Then he said to him, "Get up and go
on your way; your faith has made you well."

SILENCE

RESPONSE
Let us give thanks to the Lord our God.
~IT IS RIGHT TO GIVE GOD THANKS AND PRAISE.

CANTICLE OF THE HEROINE JUDITH (16:13–16)

ANTIPHON Great and amazing are your deeds
LORD GOD ALMIGHTY!

I will sing to my God a new song:
O Lord, you are great and glorious,
wonderful in strength, invincible.

Let all your creatures serve you,
for you spoke and they were made.
You sent out your spirit and it formed them;
there is none that can resist your voice.

For the mountains shall be shaken
to their foundations;
before your glance
the rocks shall melt like wax.

But to those who fear you
you show mercy.
For every sacrifice is a small thing,
but whoever fears the Lord is great for ever.

Glory to the Father, and to the Son,
and to the Holy Spirit:
as it was in the beginning, is now,
and will be for ever. Amen.

ANTIPHON GREAT AND AMAZING ARE YOUR DEEDS
LORD GOD ALMIGHTY!

LITANY OF THANKSGIVING
Let us give thanks to God our Father for all the gifts
so freely bestowed upon us:

For the beauty and wonder of your creation,
~We thank you, O Lord.

For all that is gracious in the lives of men and
women, revealing the image of Christ,
~We thank you, O Lord.

For our daily food and drink, our homes and
families, and our friends,
~We thank you, O Lord.

For minds to think, and hearts to love, and hands
to serve,
~We thank you, O Lord.

For health and strength to work, and leisure to
rest and play,
~We thank you, O Lord.

For the brave and courageous, who are patient in
suffering and faithful in adversity,
~We thank you, O Lord.

For valiant seekers after truth, liberty, and justice,
~We thank you, O Lord.

For the communion of saints in all times and
places,
~We thank you, O Lord.

Above all we give you thanks for the great mercies
and promises given to us in Christ Jesus our Lord;

~To him be praise and glory, with you, O
Father,
and the Holy Spirit, now and for ever. Amen.[85]

BLESSING

May the LORD bless † us and take care of us;

May the LORD be kind and gracious to us;

May the LORD look on us with favor

and give us peace.

~AMEN.

A Novena for a Healing or a Cure

Though many of the previous novenas may be used
to pray for the healing of a broken body or spirit, this
one is designed more specifically for that purpose. The
God of love is the enemy of sickness, disease, and
death. And the beloved Son he sent into the world for
our sake was famous for his healing gestures of body,
mind, and spirit.

In the name of the Father, † and of the Son,
and of the Holy Spirit.

~AMEN.

Jesus was about thirty years old

~WHEN HE BEGAN HIS WORK.

PSALM 91   GOD OUR PROTECTOR

ANTIPHON GOD WILL GIVE ANGELS CHARGE OVER
YOU.

Those who dwell in the shelter of the Most High,
who abide in the shadow of the Almighty,
will say to the Lord,
"My refuge and my fortress;
my God in whom I trust."

For the Lord will deliver you from the snares of
   the fowler
and from deadly pestilence
and will cover you with his pinions;
under the Lord's wings you will find refuge.
God's faithfulness is a shield and buckler.

You will not fear the terror of the night,
nor the arrow that flies by day,
nor the pestilence that stalks in darkness,
nor the destruction that wastes at noonday.

A thousand may fall at your side,
ten thousand at your right hand,
but it will not come near you.
You will look only with your eyes
and see the end of the wicked.

Because you have made the Lord your refuge,
the Most High your habitation,
no evil shall befall you,
no plague come near your tent.

For God will give angels charge over you
to guard you in all your ways.
They will bear you up on their hands
lest you dash your foot against a stone.
You will tread on the lion and the adder,
the young lion and the serpent you will trample
   underfoot.

Those who cling to me in love I will deliver;
I will protect them, because they know my name.

When they call me, I will answer them;
I will be with them in trouble,
I will rescue them and honor them.
I will satisfy them with long life
and show them my salvation.

ANTIPHON GOD WILL GIVE ANGELS CHARGE OVER
YOU.

PSALM PRAYER

Let us pray *(pause for quiet prayer)*:

Most High God,
from age to age until everlasting
you are our fortress and our shield.
As we find refuge under your wings,
give your angels charge over us
and deliver us from every evil and affliction.
We ask this through Christ our Lord.
~AMEN.

	JESUS CURES	MATTHEW
READING	**THE SICK**	**4:23–25**

Jesus went throughout Galilee, teaching in their
synagogues and proclaiming the good news
of the kingdom and curing every disease and
every sickness among the people. So his fame
spread throughout all Syria, and they brought to
him all the sick, those who were afflicted with
various diseases and pains, demoniacs, epileptics,
and paralytics, and he cured them. And great

crowds followed him from Galilee, the Decapolis, Jerusalem, Judea, and from beyond the Jordan.

SILENCE

RESPONSE
The people who sat in darkness
~HAVE SEEN A GREAT LIGHT.

CANTICLE OF ISAIAH THE PROPHET (12:2–6)
ANTIPHON With joy you will draw water
FROM THE WELLS OF SALVATION.

Surely God is my salvation;
I will trust, and will not be afraid,
for the LORD GOD is my strength
    and my might;
he has become my salvation.

Give thanks to the LORD,
    call on his name;
make known his deeds among the nations;
proclaim that his name is exalted.

Sing praises to the LORD,
    for he has done gloriously;
let this be known in all the earth.

Shout aloud and sing for joy,
    O royal Zion,
for great in your midst is
    the Holy One of Israel.

ANTIPHON WITH JOY YOU WILL DRAW WATER
FROM THE WELLS OF SALVATION.

Litany of the Sacred Heart of Jesus
(See pages 246–248)

Novena Prayer

Lord Jesus, healer of our souls and bodies,
during your life on earth you went about doing
good,
healing every manner of sickness and disease,
strengthening, curing, comforting, and consoling.
Healer of our broken souls and bodies
and enemy of death and disease,
lay your healing hand on *Name,*
and by your grace restore *him/her* to good health
that *he/she* may praise you without ceasing
and serve you among your holy people
for many years to come.
Blessed be Jesus, friend of the human race!
~Amen.

May God the Father bless us and keep us,
✝ God the Son lay his healing hands upon us,
God the Holy Spirit strengthen and console us.
May the Holy and Undivided Trinity guard our
body,
save our soul, and bring us in safety to our
heavenly home.
~Amen.

A Novena or Triduum for the Seriously Ill

People who are seriously ill or dying need the close attention and care of friends and relatives. Many sick people cannot pray without help from others. This devotion/novena is suggested for individual or group prayer, especially when the person is close to death. This form of prayer may also be used to prepare for the Anointing of the Sick or for Viaticum, the final reception of Holy Communion.

LEADER: In the name † of Jesus, the great
Physician of our souls and bodies.

ALL: ~AMEN.

POEM

God be in my head
   and in my understanding,
God be in my eyes
   and in my looking,
God be in my mouth
   and in my speaking,
God be in my heart
   and in my thinking,
God be at my end
   and at my departing.

Sarum Prymer, 1514[86]

PSALM 31:1–5, 7, 9–10   TRUST IN GOD[87]

ANTIPHON I place myself IN YOUR CARE, LORD.

I come to you, LORD for protection;

never let me be defeated.
You are a righteous God;
save me, I pray!
Hear me! Save me now!
Be my refuge to protect me;
my defense to save me.

You are my refuge and defense;
guide me and lead me
as you have promised.
Keep me safe from the trap
that has been set for me;
shelter me from danger.
I place myself in your care.
You will save me, LORD;
you are a faithful God.

I will be glad and rejoice
because of your constant love.
You see my suffering;
you know my trouble.

Be merciful to me, LORD,
for I am in trouble;
my eyes are tired from so much crying;
I am completely worn out.
I am exhausted by sorrow,
and weeping has shortened my life.
I am weak from all my troubles,
even my bones are wasting away.

ANTIPHON I PLACE MYSELF IN YOUR CARE, LORD.

Psalm Prayer

Let us pray *(pause for quiet prayer)*:

My rock, my stronghold,
lead me and guide me for your name's sake.
It is you who will redeem me, O Lord.
With Jesus your afflicted and dying Son,
I place myself in your care,
now and for ever.
~Amen.

	Christ	Matthew
Reading	the Healer	15:29–31

Jesus passed along the Sea of Galilee, and he went
up the mountain, where he sat down. Great crowds
came to him, bringing with them the lame, the
maimed, the blind, the mute, and many others.
They put them at his feet, and he cured them, so
that the crowd was amazed when they saw the mute
speaking, the maimed whole, the lame walking, and
the blind seeing. And they praised the God of Israel.

Silence

Response

If I should walk in the valley of darkness
~No evil would I fear.

Canticle of Daniel the Prophet (3:52–57)

Antiphon Blest be God's holy and
wonderful name!

Blest are you, God of our ancestors,
praised and glorified above all for ever!
Blest be your holy and wonderful name,
praised and glorified above all for ever!

Blest are you in your temple of glory,
praised and glorified above all for ever!
Blest are you enthroned on the cherubim,
praised and glorified above all for ever!

Blest are you who look into the depths,
praised and glorified above all for ever!
Blest are you above the vault of heaven,
praised and glorified above all for ever!

Bless the Lord, sing to God's glory,
all things fashioned by God's mighty hand.
Bless the Father, the Son, and the Holy Spirit,
praised and glorified above all for ever!

ANTIPHON BLEST BE GOD'S HOLY AND
WONDERFUL NAME!

LITANY

Lord Jesus, compassionate Son of the living God:
~HEAR US AND HELP US, WE HUMBLY PRAY.

Lord Jesus, you went about preaching repentance
and curing all kind of sickness and disease:
~HEAR US AND HELP US, WE HUMBLY PRAY.

Lord Jesus, you drove out evil spirits and healed
the insane:
~HEAR US AND HELP US, WE HUMBLY PRAY.

Lord Jesus, you cured Simon Peter's mother-in-law
of a fever and the woman who suffered from
hemorrhages:
~HEAR US AND HELP US, WE HUMBLY PRAY.

Lord Jesus, you cured lepers of their affliction
and people came to you from everywhere:
~HEAR US AND HELP US, WE HUMBLY PRAY.

Lord Jesus, you forgave a paralytic his sins,
and commanded him to take up his bed and
walk again:
~HEAR US AND HELP US, WE HUMBLY PRAY.

Lord Jesus, you cured a man with a withered arm
on the Sabbath Day:
~HEAR US AND HELP US, WE HUMBLY PRAY.

Lord Jesus, you drove out a legion of demons
from a demoniac and restored him to his right
mind:
~HEAR US AND HELP US, WE HUMBLY PRAY.

Lord Jesus, you raised the young daughter of
Jairus from the sleep of death:
~HEAR US AND HELP US, WE HUMBLY PRAY.

Lord Jesus, you delivered the tormented daughter
of the Canaanite woman
and restored the hearing of a deaf-mute:
~HEAR US AND HELP US, WE HUMBLY PRAY.

Lord Jesus, you laid your hand on the blind man
of Bethsaida and restored his sight:
~HEAR US AND HELP US, WE HUMBLY PRAY.

Lord Jesus, you restored the sight of Bartimaeus,
the blind beggar of Jericho as he sat by the
roadside:
~HEAR US AND HELP US, WE HUMBLY PRAY.

Lord Jesus, you raised to life your dear friend
Lazarus, the brother of Martha and Mary, after
he had been dead four days:
~HEAR US AND HELP US, WE HUMBLY PRAY.

Lord Jesus, you left us the Sacrament of Anointing
to comfort and console us and to prepare us
for life everlasting:
~HEAR US AND HELP US, WE HUMBLY PRAY.

(Pause for spontaneous prayers for the sick and dying.)

PRAYER
Great Physician of our souls and bodies,
you have mercy on all those who put their trust in
you.
Please heal your servant, *Name,*
of the sickness that afflicts *her/him*
and restore *her/him* to good health
to serve you in your holy Church,
now and for ever,
~AMEN.

Through the prayers of the great Mother of God,
Mary most holy, and of all the saints,
may our compassionate Lord and Savior
✝ be kind and merciful to us.
~AMEN.

A Novena for Our Dear Departed

From the very beginning Christians have prayed for the welfare of those who have gone before them with the sign of faith. This novena may be prayed for the nine days after a person's death, before or after its anniversary, on November 2, the feast of All Souls, or on any occasion of mourning.

LEADER: In the name of the Father, ✝ and of the Son, and of the Holy Spirit.

ALL: ~AMEN.

HYMN

O radiant Light, O Sun divine
Of God the Father's deathless face,
O Image of the light sublime
That fills the heavenly dwelling place;

O Son of God, the source of life,
Praise is your due by night and day;
Our happy lips must raise the strain
Of your esteemed and splendid name.

Lord Jesus Christ, as daylight fades,
As shine the lights of eventide,
We praise the Father with the Son,
The Spirit blest and with them one.

Phos Hilaron, Greek, late second century[88]

PSALM 103:1–5, 8–16   PRAISE OF GOD'S MERCY

ANTIPHON The Lord knows our frame,
AND REMEMBERS THAT WE ARE DUST.

Bless the Lord, O my soul,
and all that is within me,
bless God's holy name!

Bless the Lord, O my soul,
and forget not all God's benefits,
who forgives all your iniquity,
who heals all your diseases,

who redeems your life from the pit,
who crowns you with steadfast love and mercy,
who satisfies you with good as along as you live
so that your youth is renewed like the eagle's.

The Lord is merciful and gracious,
slow to anger and abounding in steadfast love.
The Lord will not always contend,
nor nourish anger for ever.

The Lord does not deal with us according to our
   sins,
nor repay us according to our iniquities.
For as the heavens are far above the earth,
so great is the Lord's steadfast love
   toward those who are faithful;

as far as the east is from the west,
so far the Lord removes our transgressions from
   us.
For the Lord knows our frame,
and remembers that we are dust.

As for mortals, their days are like grass;
they flourish like the flower of the field;

the wind passes over it, and it is gone,
and the field knows the flower no more.

Antiphon The Lord knows our frame,
and remembers that we are dust.

Psalm Prayer

Let us pray *(pause for quiet prayer)*:

Lord of the living and of the dead,
full of compassion and love,
you do not repay us according to our sins
but remember that we are dust in your sight.
In your everlasting love
save us by the merits of our blessed Savior,
the firstfruits of those who have died,
and awake the dwellers in the dust
that they may sing for joy,
now and for ever.
~Amen.

Awake and
Reading   **Sing for Joy**   **Isaiah 26:19**
Your dead shall live, their corpses shall rise.
O dwellers in the dust, awake and sing for joy!
For your dew is a radiant dew and the earth will
give birth to those long dead.

Silence

Response

I know that my Redeemer lives,
~And in my flesh I shall see God.

We do not live to ourselves, and we do not die to ourselves. If we live, we live to the Lord, and if we die, we die to the Lord; so then, whether we live or whether we die, we are the Lord's. For to this end Christ died and lived again, so that he might be Lord of both the dead and the living.

SILENCE

RESPONSE

Eternal rest grant to them, O Lord,
~AND LET PERPETUAL LIGHT SHINE UPON THEM.

THE SONG OF THE LAMB **REVELATION 15:3–4; 5:13**

ANTIPHON Holy is God, HOLY AND STRONG, HOLY AND LIVING FOR EVER!

Great and amazing are your deeds,
Lord God the Almighty!
Just and true are your ways,
    King of the nations!

Lord, who will not fear
    and glorify your name?
For you alone are holy.

All nations will come
and worship before you,
for your judgments have been revealed.

To the one seated on the throne
    and to the Lamb

be blessing and honor and glory and might
for ever and ever. Amen.

ANTIPHON HOLY IS GOD, HOLY AND STRONG,
HOLY AND LIVING FOR EVER!

LITANY OF THE PRECIOUS BLOOD OF JESUS
(SEE PAGES 248–251)

NOVENA PRAYER
Remembering that Jesus
shed tears at the grave of Lazarus his friend,
and as he hung on the cross
promised paradise to a repentant criminal,
we implore you, God of all consolation,
to remember your servant, *Name,*
whom you washed clean of sin
and gave new life in the waters of Baptism.
As you fed *him/her* with the precious body and
    blood of Jesus in Holy Communion,
may *she/he* rest in peace in the company
of the Blessed Virgin Mary and of all your saints,
where you live and reign, Father, Son, and Holy
    Spirit,
now and for ever.
~AMEN.

May *his/her* soul and the souls of all the faithful
    departed
through the mercy of God ✝ rest in peace.
~AMEN.

A Triduum for Holy Baptism

It is helpful to celebrate a triduum in preparation for the Baptism of an adult or a child. It is also appropriate to use this service on the eve of a Baptism or the celebration of its anniversary by parents, godparents, relatives, and friends.

LEADER: In the name † of the Father, and of the Son, and of the Holy Spirit.

ALL: ~AMEN.

BAPTISMAL HYMN   **GALATIANS 3:26–28**

In Christ Jesus
you are all children of God through faith.
As many of you as were baptized into Christ
have clothed yourselves with Christ.
There is no longer Jew or Greek,
there is no longer slave or free,
there is no longer male and female;
for all of you are one in Christ Jesus.

PSALM 8   **THE LORD OF LIFE**

ANTIPHON No one can enter the Kingdom of God
WITHOUT BEING BORN OF WATER AND THE
SPIRIT.

O Lord, our Lord,
how majestic is your name in all the earth!

Your glory is chanted above the heavens
by the mouth of babes and infants;
you have set up a defense against your foes,
to still the enemy and avenger.

When I look at the heavens, the work of your
    fingers,
the moon and the stars which you have
    established;
what are human beings that you are mindful of
    them,
and mortals that you care for them?
You have made them little less than God,
and crowned them with glory and honor.

You have given them dominion
    over the works of your hands;
you have put all things under their feet,
all sheep and oxen,
and also the beasts of the field,
the birds of the air, and the fish of the sea,
whatever passes along the paths of the sea.

O Lord, our Lord,
how majestic is your name in all the earth!

ANTIPHON NO ONE CAN ENTER THE KINGDOM OF
    GOD WITHOUT BEING BORN OF WATER AND
    THE SPIRIT.

LEADER: Let us pray *(pause for silent prayer):*
Lord of the new life,
you have created us in a dignity almost divine
and have brought us to new life
as we are born again by water and the Holy Spirit
in the sacrament of holy Baptism.

Please keep us faithful to the vows of our baptism,
and devoted members of your holy Church,
so that we may love and serve you all the days of
   our life;
through the merits of Christ our Savior.

ALL: ~AMEN.

READING NEW BIRTH TITUS 3:4–7[89]

When the kindness and love of God our Savior
was revealed, he saved us, It was not because
of any good deeds that we ourselves had done,
but because of his own mercy that he saved us,
through the Holy Spirit, who gives us new birth
and new life by washing us. God poured out the
Holy Spirit abundantly on us through Jesus Christ
our Savior, so that by his grace we might be put
right with God and come into possession of the
eternal life we hope for.

SILENCE

OR THIS READING GO AND BAPTIZE MATTHEW 28:16–20[90]

The eleven disciples went to the hill in Galilee
where Jesus had told them to go. When they saw
him, they worshiped him, even though some of
them doubted. Jesus drew near and said to them,
"I have been given all authority in heaven and
on earth. Go, then, to all peoples everywhere
and make them my disciples: baptize them in
the name of the Father, the Son, and the Holy

Spirit, and teach them to obey everything I have commanded you. And I will be with you always, to the end of the age.

(Pause for silent prayer and/or reflections.)

THE APOSTLES' CREED[91]

LEADER: Let us dedicate ourselves to the faith of the holy apostles:
I believe in God, THE FATHER ALMIGHTY, CREATOR OF HEAVEN AND EARTH.
I BELIEVE IN JESUS CHRIST, GOD'S ONLY SON, OUR LORD,
   WHO WAS CONCEIVED BY THE HOLY SPIRIT,
   BORN OF THE VIRGIN MARY,
   SUFFERED UNDER PONTIUS PILATE,
   WAS CRUCIFIED, DIED, AND WAS BURIED;
   HE DESCENDED TO THE DEAD.
   ON THE THIRD DAY HE ROSE AGAIN;
   HE ASCENDED INTO HEAVEN,
   HE IS SEATED AT THE RIGHT HAND OF THE FATHER,
   AND HE WILL COME TO JUDGE THE LIVING AND THE DEAD.
I BELIEVE IN THE HOLY SPIRIT,
   THE HOLY CATHOLIC CHURCH,
   THE COMMUNION OF SAINTS,
   THE FORGIVENESS OF SINS,
   THE RESURRECTION OF THE BODY,
   AND THE LIFE EVERLASTING. AMEN.

LITANY

Lord and life-giving Spirit, you brooded
  over the waters at the world's creation:
~MAKE US DEAD TO SIN BUT ALIVE TO GOD.

You led your people out of slavery in Egypt
  through the waters of the Red Sea:
~MAKE US DEAD TO SIN BUT ALIVE TO GOD.

You led your people Israel through the waters
  of the Jordan into the freedom of the Promised
  Land:
~MAKE US DEAD TO SIN BUT ALIVE TO GOD.

You overshadowed Mary of Nazareth
  and caused her to conceive the Son of God:
~MAKE US DEAD TO SIN BUT ALIVE TO GOD.

You anointed Jesus as Messiah and Lord
  at his baptism by John in the Jordan:
~MAKE US DEAD TO SIN BUT ALIVE TO GOD.

You raised Jesus from the grave
  and proclaimed him Son of God in all his
  power:
~MAKE US DEAD TO SIN BUT ALIVE TO GOD.

You appeared in wind and flame on Pentecost
  and touched each person there:
~MAKE US DEAD TO SIN BUT ALIVE TO GOD.

You charge the waters of baptism with power
  to give us new and everlasting life:
~MAKE US DEAD TO SIN BUT ALIVE TO GOD.

You entrust us to the Virgin Mary and to all the
saints in glory:
~Make us dead to sin but alive to God.

(Spontaneous prayer for the person to be baptized.)

The Lord's Prayer
Lord, teach us to pray.
~Our Father in heaven . . . *(Continue in unison.)*

Prayer
Almighty and everlasting God,
out of pure grace
you decreed both the creation of the world
and its renewal through the coming
of the incarnate Word of God.
Be present and active in the sacrament of rebirth
which you have instituted for our salvation.
Send forth the Spirit of adoption in full measure
that those who are born of water and the Spirit
may be your true children,
living under the power of that same Spirit
all the days of their lives.
We ask this through Jesus, our blessed Redeemer.
~Amen.

May God, the source of light and love, † be with
us all.
~Amen.

A Triduum for an Engagement to Marry

As part of any serious Christian preparation for a wedding, many couples plan a formal engagement at home or in church. This triduum may be used by the couple before the engagement proper and/or as a single event at the engagement to marry itself.

When used as an actual engagement ceremony, it is performed before an altar in church or a table at home containing a crucifix, candles, flowers, and the Holy Gospels. The leader may be a priest, deacon, or friend. The section "Promise of Future Marriage" is, of course, reserved for the engagement ceremony itself.

LEADER: In the name of the Holy and Undivided Trinity, Father, ✝ Son, and Holy Spirit.

ALL: ~AMEN.

POEM

O young, fresh folk, beloved he or she
In whom love grows, as you have grown apace,
Come home, and leave all worldly vanity;
Lift up your heart, and raise a joyous face
To God who made you, image of his grace.
And learn the fragile lesson of these hours:
This world will pass, as swift as fading flowers.

So love the God whose Christ did die for you
Upon a cross, for every soul did pay:
First died, then rose, and now in heaven stays true,
For he'll be false to none, I dare to say,

Who wholly in God's care their hearts will lay.
And since he's best to love, and is most meek,
What need is there for lesser loves to seek?

Geoffrey Chaucer (1340–1400) [92]

PSALM 127   GOD AND PARENTS

ANTIPHON You can do nothing WITHOUT ME.

Unless the Lord builds the house,
those who build it labor in vain.
Unless the Lord guards the city,
the guard keeps watch in vain.

It is vain that you rise up early
and go late to rest,
eating the bread of distressing work;
for God gives sleep to the beloved of the Lord.

Children are indeed a heritage from the Lord,
the fruit of the womb a reward.
Like arrows in the hand of a warrior
are the children of one's youth.

Happy are those who have
a quiver full of them!
They shall not be put to shame
when they speak with their enemies in the gate.

ANTIPHON YOU CAN DO NOTHING WITHOUT ME.

PSALM PRAYER

LEADER: Let us pray (*pause for quiet prayer*):

God of hope and promise,
we rely on your holy word

that promises to assist us
in the carrying out of our marriage vows.
Watch over us as we prepare
for the sacrament of marriage
and for the children that are your gift.
We ask this through Christ our Lord.
ALL: ~AMEN.

FIRST READING   A HOLY FAMILY   TOBIT 12:6–10

The angel Raphael called Tobit and Sarah privately and said to them, "Bless God and acknowledge him in the presence of all the living for the good things he has done for you. Bless and sing praise to his name. With fitting honor declare to all people the deeds of God. Do not be slow to acknowledge him. It is good to conceal the secret of a king, but to acknowledge and reveal the works of God. Do good and evil will not overtake you. Prayer with fasting is good, but better than both is almsgiving with righteousness. It is better to give alms than to lay up gold. For almsgiving saves from death and purges away every sin. Those who give alms will enjoy a full life, but those who commit sin and do wrong are their own worst enemies."

SILENCE

Then Jesus went home; and the crowd came together again, so that they could not even eat. When his family heard it, they went out to restrain him, for people were saying, "He has gone out of his mind." Then his mother and his brothers came; and standing outside, they sent to him and called him. A crowd was sitting around him; and they said to him, "Your mother and your brothers and sisters are outside, asking for you." And he replied, "Who are my mother and my brothers?" And looking at those who sat around him, he said, "Here are my mother and my brothers! Whoever does the will of God is my brother and sister and mother."

(Pause for reflections.)

Response
Blessed be God, and blessed be his great name,
~And blessed be all his holy angels.

[A Promise of Future Marriage

The couple face each other, hold hands, and make the following promises:

Man: In the sight of God and of these friends,
I promise to cherish, respect, and love you
as we prepare for our marriage in Christ.

Woman: In the sight of God and of these friends,

I promise to cherish, respect, and love you
as we prepare for our marriage in Christ.

BLESSING OF THE ENGAGEMENT RING

LEADER: Our help ✝ is in the name of the Lord,

ALL: ~THE MAKER OF HEAVEN AND EARTH.

Let us pray:

LEADER: Heavenly Father,
you established marriage in the beginning
and restored it in Christ our Savior
at the wedding feast of Cana.
Bless ✝ this ring, a sign of fidelity and
    commitment,
and after a period of serious and devout
    preparation,
bring this couple before your altar
to be united in holy wedlock.
We ask this through Christ our Lord.

ALL: ~AMEN.

The man places the ring on the woman's finger.]

LITANY

For the grace of choosing God before everything
    else, let us pray to the Lord.

~LORD, HEAR OUR PRAYER.

For the grace of God in our marriage preparation,
    let us pray to the Lord.

~LORD, HEAR OUR PRAYER.

For the gift of a true and devout family life,
    let us pray to the Lord.

~Lord, hear our prayer.

For the blessing of children, the fruit of the womb,
    let us pray to the Lord.

~Lord, hear our prayer.

For the grace to renew and keep our baptismal
    vows as we prepare for our marriage vows,
    let us pray to the Lord.

~Lord, hear our prayer.

For our parents and grandparents and other
    relations and friends, let us pray to the Lord.

~Lord, hear our prayer.

For our ancestors in the faith and all who have
    fallen asleep in Christ, *Names,* let us pray to the
    Lord.

~Lord, hear our prayer.

(Pause for intercessory prayer.)

For the loving intercession of the great Mother
    of God, Mary most holy, of our patron saints
    Names, and of all the saints, let us pray to the
    Lord.

~Lord, hear our prayer.

The Lord's Prayer

Lord, teach us to pray.

~Our Father in heaven . . . *(Continue in unison.)*

PRAYER

LEADER: Lord of creation,
in the beginning you willed that husband and wife
embrace and cherish their marital union
and thank you for this precious gift.
Please endow us with faith and wisdom
that we may walk in your ways
and be always pleasing in your sight.
We ask this through Christ our Lord,
ALL: ~AMEN.

May the LORD ✝ bless us and take care of us;
May the LORD be kind and gracious to us;
May the LORD look on us with favor
    and give us peace.
ALL: ~AMEN.

*The engaged couple may kiss the book of the
    Gospels, each other, and all present.*

A Novena in Preparation
for a Wedding

This novena can be a joyous form of preparation for the
couple and for their family and friends. It may also be
used as a devotion on the eve of the wedding and to
celebrate its anniversary.

LEADER: In the name of the Father, ✝ and of the Son,
and of the Holy Spirit.
ALL: ~AMEN.

POEM

Let all the world in every corner sing:
My God and King!
The heavens are not too high,
His praises there may fly;
The earth is not too low,
His praises there may grow.
Let all the world in every corner sing:
My God and King!

Let all the world in every corner sing:
My God and King!
The Church with psalms must shout,
No door can keep them out;
But, more than all, the heart
Must bear the longest part.
Let all the world in every corner sing:
My God and King!

George Herbert (1593–1633)

PSALM 128   A HAPPY HOME AND LONG LIFE

ANTIPHON Blessed is everyone WHO WALKS IN
GOD'S WAYS!

Blessed is everyone who fears the Lord,
who walks in God's ways.

You shall eat the fruit of the labor of your hands;
you shall be happy,
and it shall go well with you.
Your wife will be like a fruitful vine
within your house;

your children will be like olive shoots
around your table.

Thus shall those be blessed
who fear the Lord.
The Lord bless you from Zion!
May you see the prosperity of Jerusalem
all the days of your life.
May you see your children's children.
Peace be upon Israel!

ANTIPHON BLESSED IS EVERYONE WHO WALKS IN
GOD'S WAYS!

PSALM PRAYER
LEADER: Let us pray *(pause for quiet prayer)*:

Abba, dear Father,
bless our coming wedding and marriage
and help us walk together in peace and beauty
all the days of our life.
We ask this through Christ our Lord.
ALL: ~AMEN.

| | **GOD** | **MALACHI** |
| **READING** | **HATES DIVORCE** | **2:13–16** |

You cover the LORD's altar with tears, with
weeping and groaning because he no longer
regards the offering or accepts it with favor at
your hand. You ask, "Why does he not?" Because
the LORD was a witness between you and the wife
of your youth, to whom you have been faithless,

though she is your companion and your wife by covenant. Did not one God make her? Both flesh and spirit are his. And what does the one God desire? Godly offspring. So look to yourselves, and do not let anyone be faithless to the wife of his youth. For I hate divorce, says the LORD.

SILENCE

OR THIS READING   **NO DIVORCE**   **MARK 10:2–9**

Some Pharisees came, and to test Jesus they asked, "Is it lawful for a man to divorce his wife?" He answered them, "What did Moses command you?" They said, "Moses allowed a man to write a certificate of dismissal and to divorce her." But Jesus said to them, "Because of your hardness of heart he wrote this commandment for you. But from the beginning of creation, 'God made them male and female.' 'For this reason a man shall leave his father and mother and be joined to his wife, and the two shall become one flesh.' So they are no longer two, but one flesh. Therefore what God has joined together, let no one separate."

SILENCE

RESPONSE

Then God said, "And now we will make human beings;

~THEY WILL BE LIKE US AND RESEMBLE US."

A Novena in Preparation for a Wedding **239**

CANTICLE OF THE VIRGIN MARY   LUKE 1:46–55[93]

ANTIPHON Mother of God AND WOMAN FULL
OF GRACE, YOU CARRIED IN YOUR WOMB THE
LORD OF GLORY!

My soul † proclaims the greatness of the Lord,
my spirit rejoices in God my Savior,
for you, Lord, have looked with favor on your
    lowly servant.

From this day all generations will call me blessed:
    you, the Almighty, have done great things for
    me and holy is your name.
    You have mercy on those who fear you,
    from generation to generation.

You have shown strength with your arm
and scattered the proud in their conceit,
casting down the mighty from their thrones
    and lifting up the lowly.
You have filled the hungry with good things
and sent the rich away empty.

You have come to the aid of your servant Israel,
to remember the promise of mercy,
the promise made to our forebears,
to Abraham and his children for ever.

Glory to the Father, and to the Son,
and to the Holy Spirit:
as it was in the beginning, is now,
and will be for ever. Amen.

ANTIPHON MOTHER OF GOD AND WOMAN FULL
OF GRACE, YOU CARRIED IN YOUR WOMB THE
LORD OF GLORY!

LITANY

In peace, let us pray to the Lord.
~LORD, HEAR OUR PRAYER.

For peace from on high and for the salvation of
our souls, let us pray to the Lord.
~LORD, HEAR OUR PRAYER.

For the peace of the whole world, the welfare
of the Universal Church, and for the unity
of the human race, let us pray to the Lord.
~LORD, HEAR OUR PRAYER.

For this nation and its government and for all who
serve and protect us, let us pray to the Lord.
~LORD, HEAR OUR PRAYER.

For this Christian couple, *Name* and *Name,* who
marry in Christ, let us pray to the Lord.
~LORD, HEAR OUR PRAYER.

For the gift of children and the peace and unity of
our family, let us pray to the Lord.
~LORD, HEAR OUR PRAYER.

For parents and grandparents and all our friends
and relatives, let us pray to the Lord.
~LORD, HEAR OUR PRAYER.

For our deliverance from all affliction, danger,
and need, let us pray to the Lord.
~LORD, HEAR OUR PRAYER.

For our beloved dead who have fallen asleep in
Christ, *Names,* let us pray to the Lord.
~LORD, HEAR OUR PRAYER.

Help, save, pity, and defend us, O Lord, by your
grace.
~LORD, HEAR OUR PRAYER.

(Pause for intercessory prayer.)

Rejoicing in the memory of the Blessed Virgin
Mary, of Saints *Name* and *Name,* and of all the
saints, let us commend ourselves, one another,
and our whole life to Christ our Lord.
ALL: ~TO YOU, O LORD.

PRAYER
By your grace, O God,
we come before you with confidence
in your promise that you will grant the requests
of those gathered together in your name.
Please grant the united prayers of this couple
and their friends and relatives,
granting them in this world knowledge of your
holy will
and in the world to come life everlasting.
All glory, honor, and worship are your due,
Father, Son, and Holy Spirit,
now and always and for ever and ever.

ALL: ~Amen.

BLESSING

LEADER: May the Lord ✝ bless us and take care of
us;

May the Lord be kind and gracious to us;

May the Lord look upon us with favor
and give us peace.

ALL: ~Amen.

The couple may kiss the Book of the Gospels, each
other, and all present.

Litanies and Insistent Prayer

In both the Eastern and Western liturgical families, litanies are an ancient form of repetitive, intercessory prayer, originally designed for the Eucharistic Liturgy and the Daily Office. Such litanies are led by a deacon who formulates the petitions, and the congregation answers with a simple response: "Kyrie, eleison:" "Lord, have mercy" or "Lord, hear our prayer."

In recent years many churches have revived the use of litanies in the Eucharist and in daily Morning and Evening Prayer, A litany helps us to pray earnestly and urgently for the Church and the world as an expression of faith in Jesus' words: "Ask, and it will be given you; search, and you will find; knock, and the door will be opened for you" (Matthew 7:7).

In popular devotions like novenas and triduums, litanies are a beautiful and powerful form of intercessory prayer, forceful reminders of the central mysteries of the faith. In brief phrases from the Bible, the Liturgy, and Christian poetry, they bring to mind before God motives for faith, trust, devotion, love, and adoration as we ask for mercy and assistance. Good examples of such litanies are those of the Sacred Heart of Jesus, the Precious Blood of Jesus, the Blessed Sacrament, the Blessed Virgin Mary, and Saint Joseph.

Those who are pressed for time might consider using one of the following litanies by itself as a form of intercession over three or nine days.

Litany of the Sacred Heart of Jesus

Lord, have mercy.	~LORD, HAVE MERCY.
Christ, have mercy.	~CHRIST, HAVE MERCY.
Lord, have mercy.	~LORD, HAVE MERCY.

God our Father in heaven,	~HAVE MERCY ON US.
God the Son, Redeemer of the world,	~HAVE MERCY ON US.
God the Holy Spirit,	~HAVE MERCY ON US.
Holy Trinity, one God,	~HAVE MERCY ON US.

Heart of Jesus, Son of the eternal Father,	~HAVE MERCY ON US.
Heart of Jesus, formed by the Holy Spirit in the womb of the Virgin Mother,	~HAVE MERCY ON US.
Heart of Jesus, one with the eternal Word,	~HAVE MERCY ON US.
Heart of Jesus, infinite in majesty,	~HAVE MERCY ON US.
Heart of Jesus, holy temple of God,	~HAVE MERCY ON US.
Heart of Jesus, tabernacle of the Most High,	~HAVE MERCY ON US.
Heart of Jesus, house of God and gate of heaven,	~HAVE MERCY ON US.

Heart of Jesus, aflame with love for us,	~HAVE MERCY ON US.
Heart of Jesus, source of justice and love,	~HAVE MERCY ON US.
Heart of Jesus, full of goodness and love,	~HAVE MERCY ON US.

Heart of Jesus, wellspring of all
virtue, ~HAVE MERCY ON US.

Heart of Jesus, worthy of all
praise, ~HAVE MERCY ON US.

Heart of Jesus, king and center
of all hearts, ~HAVE MERCY ON US.

Heart of Jesus, treasure-house of
wisdom and knowledge, ~HAVE MERCY ON US.

Heart of Jesus, in whom there
dwells the fullness of God, ~HAVE MERCY ON US.

Heart of Jesus, in whom the
Father is well pleased, ~HAVE MERCY ON US.

Heart of Jesus, of whose fullness
we have all received, ~HAVE MERCY ON US.

Heart of Jesus, desire of the
eternal hills, ~HAVE MERCY ON US.

Heart of Jesus, patient and full
of mercy, ~HAVE MERCY ON US.

Heart of Jesus, generous to all
who turn to you, ~HAVE MERCY ON US.

Heart of Jesus, fountain of life
and holiness, ~HAVE MERCY ON US.

Heart of Jesus, atonement for our
sins, ~HAVE MERCY ON US.

Heart of Jesus, overwhelmed with
insults, ~HAVE MERCY ON US.

Heart of Jesus, broken for our sins, ~HAVE MERCY ON US.

Heart of Jesus, obedient even to
death, ~HAVE MERCY ON US.

Heart of Jesus, pierced by a lance, ~HAVE MERCY ON US.

Heart of Jesus, source of all
consolation, ~HAVE MERCY ON US.

Heart of Jesus, our life and
resurrection, ~HAVE MERCY ON US.

Heart of Jesus, our peace and
reconciliation, ~HAVE MERCY ON US.
Heart of Jesus, victim for our sins, ~HAVE MERCY ON US.
Heart of Jesus, salvation of all
who trust in you, ~HAVE MERCY ON US.
Heart of Jesus, hope of all who
die in you, ~HAVE MERCY ON US.
Heart of Jesus, delight of all
the saints, ~HAVE MERCY ON US.

(Pause for spontaneous prayer.)

Lamb of God, you take away
the sins of the world, ~HAVE MERCY ON US.
Lamb of God, you take away
the sins of the world, ~HAVE MERCY ON US.
Lamb of God, you take away
the sins of the world, ~HAVE MERCY ON US.

Jesus, gentle and humble of heart,
~TOUCH OUR HEARTS AND MAKE THEM LIKE YOUR OWN.

Let us pray:

Father,
we rejoice in the gifts of love
we have received from the heart of Jesus your Son.
Open our hearts to share his life
and continue to bless us with his love.
We ask this in the name of Jesus the Lord.
~AMEN.[94]

Litany of the
Precious Blood of Jesus

Lord, have mercy. ~LORD, HAVE MERCY.
Christ, have mercy. ~CHRIST, HAVE MERCY.
Lord, have mercy. ~LORD, HAVE MERCY.

God our Father in heaven, ~Have mercy on us.
God the Son, Redeemer
    of the world, ~Have mercy on us.
God the Holy Spirit, ~Have mercy on us.
Holy Trinity, one God, ~Have mercy on us.

Blood of Christ, only Son of the
    Father, ~Be our salvation.
Blood of Christ, incarnate Word, ~Be our salvation.
Blood of Christ, of the new and
    eternal covenant, ~Be our salvation.
Blood of Christ, that spilled to the
    ground, ~Be our salvation.
Blood of Christ, that flowed at the
    scourging, ~Be our salvation.
Blood of Christ, dripping from
    the thorns, ~Be our salvation.
Blood of Christ, shed on the cross, ~Be our salvation.
Blood of Christ, the price of our
    redemption, ~Be our salvation.
Blood of Christ, our only claim to
    pardon, ~Be our salvation.
Blood of Christ, our blessing cup, ~Be our salvation.
Blood of Christ, in which we are
    washed, ~Be our salvation.
Blood of Christ, torrent of mercy, ~Be our salvation.
Blood of Christ, that overcomes
    evil, ~Be our salvation.
Blood of Christ, strength of the
    martyrs, ~Be our salvation.
Blood of Christ, endurance of the
    saints, ~Be our salvation.
Blood of Christ, that makes the
    barren fruitful, ~Be our salvation.

Blood of Christ, protection of the
threadened, ~BE OUR SALVATION.

Blood of Christ, comfort of the
weary, ~BE OUR SALVATION.

Blood of Christ, solace of the
mourner, ~BE OUR SALVATION.

Blood of Christ, hope of the
repentant, ~BE OUR SALVATION.

Blood of Christ, consolation of
the dying, ~BE OUR SALVATION.

Blood of Christ, our peace and
refreshment, ~BE OUR SALVATION.

Blood of Christ, our pledge of life, ~BE OUR SALVATION.

Blood of Christ, by which we pass
to glory, ~BE OUR SALVATION.

Blood of Christ, most worthy of
honor, ~BE OUR SALVATION.

(Pause for spontaneous prayer.)

Lamb of God, you take away
the sins of the world, ~HAVE MERCY ON US.

Lamb of God, you take away
the sins of the world, ~HAVE MERCY ON US.

Lamb of God, you take away
the sins of the world, ~HAVE MERCY ON US.

Lord, you redeemed us by your blood.
~YOU HAVE MADE US A KINGDOM TO SERVE OUR GOD.

Let us pray:

Father,
by the blood of your Son
you have set us free and saved us from death.
Continue your work of love within us,
that by constantly celebrating the mystery of our salvation
we may reach the eternal life it promises.

We ask this through Christ our Lord.
~AMEN.[95]

Litany of the
Blessed Sacrament of the Altar

Lord, have mercy.	~LORD, HAVE MERCY.
Christ, have mercy.	~CHRIST, HAVE MERCY.
Lord, have mercy.	~LORD, HAVE MERCY.
God our Father in heaven,	~HAVE MERCY ON US.
God the Son, Redeemer of the world,	~HAVE MERCY ON US.
God the Holy Spirit,	~HAVE MERCY ON US.
Holy Trinity, one God,	~HAVE MERCY ON US.
Word made flesh and living among us,	~CHRIST, HAVE MERCY ON US.
Pure and acceptable sacrifice,	~CHRIST, HAVE MERCY ON US.
Hidden manna from above,	~CHRIST, HAVE MERCY ON US.
Living bread that came down from heaven,	~CHRIST, HAVE MERCY ON US.
Bread of life for a hungry world,	~CHRIST, HAVE MERCY ON US.
Chalice of blessing,	~CHRIST, HAVE MERCY ON US.
Precious blood that washes away our sins,	~CHRIST, HAVE MERCY ON US.
Memorial of God's undying love,	~CHRIST, HAVE MERCY ON US.
Food that lasts for eternal life,	~CHRIST, HAVE MERCY ON US.
Mystery of faith,	~CHRIST, HAVE MERCY ON US.
Medicine of immortality,	~CHRIST, HAVE MERCY ON US.
Food of God's chosen,	~CHRIST, HAVE MERCY ON US.

Perpetual presence in our
tabernacles, ~CHRIST, HAVE MERCY ON US.
Viaticum of those who die
in the Lord, ~CHRIST, HAVE MERCY ON US.
Pledge of future glory, ~CHRIST, HAVE MERCY ON US.

Be merciful, ~SPARE US, GOOD LORD.
Be merciful, ~GRACIOUSLY HEAR US, GOOD LORD.

By the great longing you had to
eat the Passover with your
disciples, ~GOOD LORD, DELIVER US.
By your humility in washing
their feet, ~GOOD LORD, DELIVER US.
By your loving gift of this
divine sacrament, ~GOOD LORD, DELIVER US.
By the five wounds of your
precious body, ~GOOD LORD, DELIVER US.
By your sacrificial death on
the cross, ~GOOD LORD, DELIVER US.
By the piercing of your sacred
heart, ~GOOD LORD, DELIVER US.
By your rising to new life, ~GOOD LORD, DELIVER US.
By your gift of the Holy
Spirit, our advocate
and guide, ~GOOD LORD, DELIVER US.
By your return in glory to
judge the living and the
dead, ~GOOD LORD, DELIVER US.

(Pause for spontaneous prayer.)

Lamb of God, you take away
the sins of the world, ~HAVE MERCY ON US.
Lamb of God, you take away
the sins of the world, ~HAVE MERCY ON US.
Lamb of God, you take away
the sins of the world, ~HAVE MERCY ON US.

You gave them bread from heaven to be their food.
~AND THIS BREAD CONTAINED ALL GOODNESS.

Let us pray:

Lord Jesus Christ,
you gave us the Eucharist
as the memorial of your suffering and death.
May our worship of this sacrament of your Body
   and Blood
help us to experience the salvation you won for us
and the peace of your kingdom,
where you live with the Father and the Holy Spirit,
one God for ever and ever.
~AMEN. [96]

Litany of Loreto

Lord, have mercy.	~LORD, HAVE MERCY.
Christ, have mercy.	~CHRIST, HAVE MERCY.
Lord, have mercy.	~LORD, HAVE MERCY.

God our Father in heaven,	~HAVE MERCY ON US.
God the Son, Redeemer of the world,	~HAVE MERCY ON US.
God the Holy Spirit,	~HAVE MERCY ON US.
Holy Trinity, one God,	~HAVE MERCY ON US.

Holy Mary,	~PRAY FOR US.
Holy Mother of God,	~PRAY FOR US.
Most honored of virgins,	~PRAY FOR US.

Mother of Christ,	~PRAY FOR US.
Mother of the Church,	~PRAY FOR US.
Mother of divine grace,	~PRAY FOR US.
Mother most pure,	~PRAY FOR US.
Mother of chaste love,	~PRAY FOR US.
Mother and virgin,	~PRAY FOR US.

Sinless Mother,	~Pray for us.
Dearest of mothers,	~Pray for us.
Model of motherhood,	~Pray for us.
Mother of good counsel,	~Pray for us.
Mother of our Creator,	~Pray for us.
Mother of our Savior,	~Pray for us.
Virgin most wise,	~Pray for us.
Virgin rightly praised,	~Pray for us.
Virgin rightly renowned,	~Pray for us.
Virgin most powerful,	~Pray for us.
Virgin gentle in mercy,	~Pray for us.
Faithful virgin,	~Pray for us.
Mirror of justice,	~Pray for us.
Throne of wisdom,	~Pray for us.
Cause of our joy,	~Pray for us.
Shrine of the Spirit,	~Pray for us.
Glory of Israel,	~Pray for us.
Vessel of selfless devotion,	~Pray for us.
Mystical rose,	~Pray for us.
Tower of David,	~Pray for us.
Tower of ivory,	~Pray for us.
House of gold,	~Pray for us.
Ark of the Covenant,	~Pray for us.
Gate of heaven,	~Pray for us.
Morning star,	~Pray for us.
Health of the sick,	~Pray for us.
Refuge of sinners,	~Pray for us.
Comfort of the troubled,	~Pray for us.
Help of Christians,	~Pray for us.
Queen of angels,	~Pray for us.
Queen of patriarchs and prophets,	~Pray for us.
Queen of apostles and martyrs,	~Pray for us.
Queen of confessors and virgins,	~Pray for us.

Queen of all saints,	~PRAY FOR US.
Queen conceived in grace,	~PRAY FOR US.
Queen raised up to glory,	~PRAY FOR US.
Queen of the rosary,	~PRAY FOR US.
Queen of peace,	~PRAY FOR US.

(Pause for spontaneous prayer.)

Lamb of God, you take away the sins of the world,	~HAVE MERCY ON US.
Lamb of God, you take away the sins of the world,	~HAVE MERCY ON US.
Lamb of God, you take away the sins of the world,	~HAVE MERCY ON US.

Pray for us, holy Mother of God,
~THAT WE MAY BECOME WORTHY OF THE PROMISES
OF CHRIST.

Let us pray:

Eternal God,
let your people enjoy constant health in mind and body.
Through the intercession of the Virgin Mary
free us from the sorrows of this life
and lead us to happiness in the life to come.
Grant this through Christ our Lord.
~AMEN.[97]

Litany of St. Joseph

Lord, have mercy.	~LORD, HAVE MERCY.
Christ, have mercy.	~CHRIST, HAVE MERCY.
Lord, have mercy.	~LORD, HAVE MERCY.
God our Father in heaven,	~HAVE MERCY ON US.
God the Son, Redeemer of the world,	~HAVE MERCY ON US.

| God the Holy Spirit, | ~HAVE MERCY ON US. |
| Holy Trinity, one God, | ~HAVE MERCY ON US. |

Holy Mary,	~PRAY FOR US.
St. Joseph,	~PRAY FOR US.
Noble son of the House of David,	~PRAY FOR US.
Light of patriarchs,	~PRAY FOR US.
Husband of the Mother of God,	~PRAY FOR US.
Guardian of the Virgin,	~PRAY FOR US.
Foster father of the Son of God,	~PRAY FOR US.
Faithful guardian of Christ,	~PRAY FOR US.
Head of the holy family,	~PRAY FOR US.

Joseph, chaste and just,	~PRAY FOR US.
Joseph, prudent and brave,	~PRAY FOR US.
Joseph, obedient and loyal,	~PRAY FOR US.
Pattern of patience,	~PRAY FOR US.
Lover of poverty,	~PRAY FOR US.
Model of workers,	~PRAY FOR US.
Example to parents,	~PRAY FOR US.
Guardian of virgins,	~PRAY FOR US.
Pillar of family life,	~PRAY FOR US.
Comfort of the troubled,	~PRAY FOR US.
Hope of the sick,	~PRAY FOR US.
Patron of the dying,	~PRAY FOR US.
Terror of evil spirits,	~PRAY FOR US.
Protector of the Church,	~PRAY FOR US.

(Pause for spontaneous prayer.)

Lamb of God, you take away the sins of the world,	~HAVE MERCY ON US.
Lamb of God, you take away the sins of the world,	~HAVE MERCY ON US.
Lamb of God, you take away the sins of the world,	~HAVE MERCY ON US.

God made him master of his household.
~AND PUT HIM IN CHARGE OF ALL THAT HE OWNED.

Let us pray:

Almighty God,
in your infinite wisdom and love
you chose Joseph to be the husband of Mary,
the mother of your Son.
As we enjoy his protection on earth
may we have the help of his prayers in heaven.
We ask this through Christ our Lord.
~AMEN.[98]

A Paraphrase of the Lord's Prayer

OUR FATHER IN HEAVEN:
HALLOWED BE YOUR NAME—
Your name is holy above all other names
and must be worshipped above all other names,
and especially by me your child of grace.
May I live and act so as to hallow your name
in the sight of all.

YOUR KINGDOM COME—
May your kingdom be my life's center,
the principal point of my desires.
Let it be to me a state of grace here and now
and a state of glory in the world to come.

YOUR WILL BE DONE ON EARTH AS IN HEAVEN—
Let self-will depart from me.
Let your holy and gracious will

be done in me and by me,
as it is in heaven by saints and angels.

GIVE US TODAY OUR DAILY BREAD—

Give me what I need for health and peace.
Fix my heart on things above, not on things on
    earth.
Give me the bread from heaven for my salvation.

FORGIVE US OUR SINS—

Forgive me my debts, the huge sum of debts,
shameful falls, frequent relapses, daily wallowings.
With God there is mercy and plenteous
    redemption.

AS WE FORGIVE THOSE WHO SIN AGAINST US—

Help me to love my enemies
and pray for those who mistreat and persecute me.
Teach me to forgive as I am forgiven.

SAVE US FROM THE TIME OF TRIAL—

Mindful of my frailty,
save me from trial and temptation
and be my Savior on the great and final day.

AND DELIVER US FROM EVIL—

From the world, the flesh, and the devil.
From the evils of the present age
and of the age to come.

FOR THE KINGDOM, THE POWER, AND THE GLORY ARE YOURS, NOW AND FOR EVER. AMEN.[99]

Notes

1. *Directory of Popular Piety and the Liturgy* (Vatican City, December 17, 2001), 158.
2. Text: Stanbrook Abbey, Callow End, Worcester, WR2 4TD.
3. English Language Liturgical Consultation (hereafter cited as "ELLC"), *Praying Together* (Nashville: Abingdon Press, 1988).
4. *Trinity Sunday,* alternative prayer, ICEL.
5. Text adapted from Edward Caswall (1814–1878), from *Saevo dolorum turbine,* Roman Breviary (Bologna, 1827); this version © Panel of Monastic Musicians, Mount Saint Bernard Abbey, Coalville, Leicester LE67 5UL, UK.
6. Attributed to Thomas à Kempis (c. 1380–c. 1471), trans. John Mason Neale (1851).
7. Saint Augustine of Hippo in *Directory of Popular Piety and the Liturgy* (Vatican City, December 17, 2001), 168.
8. Text: *Quicumque certum quaeritis,* eighteenth century, trans. Edward Caswall (1814–1878), alt.
9. TEV.
10. *A New Zealand Prayer Book* (hereafter cited as "NZPB") (Christchurch, New Zealand: Genesis Publications, 2002), 77.
11. *Showings* (long text), chap. 12 (New York: Paulist Press, 1978), 200.
12. Text: *Pange lingua gloriosi,* St. Thomas Aquinas, O.P. (1225–1274), trans. James Quinn, S.J., in *Praise for All Seasons* (Pittsburgh: Selah Publ., 1994), 59.

13. ICEL, alt. collect.

14. Christina Rossetti (1830–1894).

15. ELLC.

16. Clement of Rome, *Epistle to the Corinthians,* 16, 1–2, trans. James A. Kleist, S.J., in *The Epistles of St. Clement of Rome* (Westminster, MD: Newman Bookshop, 1946), 18. Cf. Isaiah 53.

17. St. Patrick's *Lorica,* trans. Cecil Francis Alexander (1818–1895).

18. TEV.

19. TEV.

20. Carl P. Daw, Jr (1944–), © 1982 Hope Publishing Co., administered in the U.K. by CopyCare.

21. Byzantine Liturgy, translated by William G. Storey.

22. TEV.

23. *Directory,* 188.

24. *Ave, Regina caelorum,* trans. James Quinn, S.J., in *Praise for All Seasons* (Pittsburgh: Selah Pub., 1994), 99.

25. ELLC.

26. Lawrence Cunningham, *Mother of God* (New York: Scala Books, 1982).

27. *Book of Mary* (Washington, DC: BCL, 1987), 19.

28. *Directory,* 183.

29. Text: *Maria aurora,* trans. Paul Cross, 1949, alt.

30. TEV.

31. ICEL, alternate prayer for Corpus Christi.

32. *Nican Mopohua,* 22–23, trans. Virgil Elizondo, in *Guadalupe, Mother of the New Creation* (Maryknoll, NY: Orbis Books, 1998), 7–8.

33. *Alma Redemptoris Mater,* trans. James Quinn, S.J., in *Praise for All Seasons* (Pittsburgh: Selah Pub. Co, 1994), 97.

34. TEV.

35. ELLC.

36. *A Book of Prayers* (Washington, DC: ICEL, 1982), 34.

37. Feast of Our Lady of Guadalupe, December 12, ICEL.

38. James Quinn, S.J., *Praise for All Seasons* (Pittsburgh: Selah Publ., 1994), 16. (See also John 19:26–27, 34; Genesis 2:21–24; Ephesians 5:25–27.)

39. ELLC.

40. James Quinn, S.J., *Praise for All Seasons* (Pittsburgh: Selah Publ., 1994), 97. (See also Isaiah 35:1–2, 5–10.)

41. TEV.

42. ELLC.

43. *Salve Regina,* eleventh century, trans. James Quinn, S.J., in *Praise for All Seasons* (Pittsburgh: Selah Publ., 1994), 96.

44. ELLC.

45. Traditional Scottish Gaelic folk prayer, trans. Kenneth H. Jones, in *A Celtic Miscellany* (Harmondsworth: Penguin Books, 1982), 305.

46. TEV.

47. ELLC.

48. *Directory,* # 174.

49. Anonymous, alt. © 1995, Panel of Monastic Musicians, Mount Saint Bernard Abbey, Coalville, Leicester, LE67 5UL, # 414.

50. TEV.

51. ELLC.

52. *O gloriosa femina,* attributed to Venantius Fortunatus (530–609), trans. John Mason Neale (1818–1866), alt.

53. Adapted from several medieval manuscripts of the twelfth and thirteenth centuries; translated by William G. Storey.

54. *A Book of Prayers* (Washington, DC: ICEL, 1982), 35.

55. Romano Guardini, *The Lord* (Chicago: Henry Regnery, 1954), 24.

56. Text: © 1974, Stanbrook Abbey, Callow End, Worcester WR2 4TD.

57. ELLC.

58. *The Book of Alernative Services* (Toronto, Ontario: Anglican Book Centre, 1985), 410–11.

59. James Quinn, S.J., *Praise for All Seasons* (Pittsburgh: Selah Publ., 1994), 106.

60. Walter Hilton, *The Scale of Perfection,* book 2, chapter 46, trans. John P. H. Clark and Rosemary Dorward (New York: Paulist Press, 1991), 300–301.

61. Text: John Mason Neale (1818–1866), alt. from *Tibi, Christe, splendor Patris* (tenth century); *Hymns for Prayer and Praise,* #440.

62. Text: *The Canticle of All Creatures* by Francis of Assisi, trans. by The Community of St. Clare, Freeland, Oxford OX8 8AJ.

63. Translated by William G. Storey.

64. Caroline Maria Noel (1817–1877).

65. Translated and alt. by William G. Storey.

66. Text: © 1995, Panel of Monastic Musicians, Mount Saint Bernard Abbey, Coalville, Leicester LE67 5UL.

67. ELLC.

68. Charles Wesley, "The Whole Armor of God," in *Wesleyan Hymn Book of 1780.*

69. Mother Teresa in Eileen Egan, *Such a Vision of the Street* (New York: Doubleday, 1985), 396–97.

70. Text: *Fortem virile pectore,* Silvio Antoniano (1540–1603), trans. Roger Nachtwey, 1964; Copyright belongs to The Lorenz Corp., POB 802, Dayton, OH 45401.

71. NZPB. 82–83.

72. *Lorica,* attributed to St. Patrick of Ireland (ca. 386–460), trans. Cecil Frances Alexander (1818–1895).

73. ELLC.

74. St. Patrick's *Lorica,* trans. by Cecil Frances Alexander (1818–1895).

75. ELLC. From her childhood years in Chicago, Dorothy Day memorized the *Te Deum* and recited it for the rest of her life.

76. Text: © 1974 and 1995, Stanbrook Abbey, Callow End, Worcester, WR2 4TD.

77. Dorothee Soelle, *Stations of the Cross, A Latin American Pilgrimage* (Minneapolis, MN: Augsburg Fortress Press, 1993), 74–75.

78. Text from *Rex gloriose martyrum* (sixth century), © 1971 John Webster Grant, alt.

79. ELLC.

80. John S. B. Monsell (1811–1875), alt.

81. Translated by William G. Storey.

82. Attributed to St. Patrick of Ireland (c. 389–c. 461), trans. Cecil Frances Alexander.

83. Text: *Quicumque certum quaeritis,* eighteenth century Latin hymn, trans. Edward Caswall (1814–1878), in *Lyra Catholica,* 849, alt.

84. Text: *Nun danket alle Gott,* Martin Rinkart (1586–1649), trans. Catherine Winkworth (1827–1878).

85. *The Book of Common Prayer* (New York: Seabury Press, 1979), 837.

86. Translated by William G. Storey.

87. TEV.

88. Translated by William G. Storey.

89. TEV.

90. TEV.

91. ELLC.

92. Geoffrey Chaucer (1340–1400), *Troilus and Criseyde,* line 1835f, translated by Dolores Warwick Frese, professor of English, the University of Notre Dame. Used with permission.

93. ELLC.

94. *Book of Prayers* (Washington, DC: ICEL, 1982), 24–25. Most of the invocations in this litany can be traced to the seventeenth century. The litany was approved by Pope Leo XIII (1810–1903).

95. *Book of Prayers,* 26–27. This litany was approved for the Universal Church by Pope John XXIII on February 24, 1960.

96. The invocations in this litany are drawn from several nineteenth- and twentieth-century prayer books.

97. *Book of Prayers*, 28–29. A Marian litany containing some of these invocations was in use in the twelfth century. It was recorded in its present form (apart from a few additions by recent popes) at the Marian shrine of Loreto (Italy) in 1558 and approved by Pope Sixtus V (1521–1590).

98. *Book of Prayers*, 30–31. Approved by Pope Pius X (1835–1914).

99. Lancelot Andrewes (1555–1626), alt.

Acknowledgments cont.

Psalms for Praise and Worship ed. Holbert, et al. © 1992 by Abingdon Press. Used by permission.

"Eternal Trinity of love," "God called great prohets," and "Martyrs living now with Christ" © Stanbrook Abbey 1974.

The text of the Alternative Opening Prayers for Trinity Sunday and Corpus Christi from *The Roman Missal* © 1973, International Committee on English in the Liturgy, Inc. (ICEL); the English translation of Litany of the Sacred heart, Litany of the Precious blood, Litany of St. Joseph, Litany of Loretto, the *Memorare,* and the Ancient Prayers to the Virgin *Sub tuum praesidium)* from *A Book of Prayers* © 1982, ICEL. All rights reserved.

Selections from *The Psalms: Grail Translation from the Hebrew* © 1993 By the Ladies of the Grail (England). Used by permission of GIA Publications, Inc. All rights reserved. Printed in U.S.A. 7404 S. Mason Ave., Chicago, IL 60638. www.giamusic.com. 800.442.1358.

Copyright material taken from "A New Zealand Prayer Book: He Karakia Mihinare O Aotearoa" is used with permission.

Hail Our Savior's Glorious Body
Text: Pange, lingua, gloriosi Corporis, St. Thomas Aquinas; para. James Quin, SJ. Text © James Quinn, SJ, Selah Publishing Co., Inc., North American agent. www.selahpub.com. Used by permission. License no. 24131.

Lide the Murmur of a Dove's Song
Words: Carl P. Daw, Jr.
Words © 1982 Hope Publishing Co., Carol Stream, IL 60188
All rights reserved. Used by permission.

"O Queen of Heav'n, to You the Angels Sing"
Text: Ave, Regina coelorum; para. James Quinn, SJ. Text © James Quinn, SJ, Selah Publishing Co., Inc., North American agent. www.selahpub.com. Used by permission. License no. 24131.

"Akathist Hymn" from MOTHER OF GOD by LAWRENCE CUNNINGHAM and PHOTOGRAPHS BY NICOLAS SAPIEHA
Copyright © 1982 by Lawrence Cunningham. Illustrations copyright © 1982 by Scala.
Reprinted by permission of HarperCollins Publishers Inc.

"Mother of Christ, Our Hope, Our Patroness"
Text: James Quinn, SJ. © James Quinn, SJ. Used by permission of Selah Publishing Co., Inc., North American agent. www.selahpub.com. Used by permission. License no. 24131.

"The New Eve Stands Before the Tree"
Text: James Quinn, SJ. Text © James Quinn, SJ, Selah Publishing Co., Inc., North American agent. www.selahpub.com. Used by permission. License no. 24131.

"Mary of Carmel, Crowned with Heaven's Glory"
Text: James Quinn, SJ. Text © James Quinn, SJ, Selah Publishing Co., Inc., North American agent. www.selahpub.com. Used by permission. License no. 24131.

"Hail, Our Queen and Mother Blest"
Text: Salve Regina, para. James Quinn, SJ. Text © James Quinn, SJ, Selah Publishing Co., Inc., North American agent. www.selahpub.com. Used by permission. License no. 24131.

Excerpts from *The Book of Alternative Services* © copyright 1985 by the General Synod of the Anglican Church of Canada. Used with permission.

"Joseph, We Praise You"
Text: James Quinn, SJ. Text © James Quinn, SJ, Selah Publishing Co., Inc., North American agent. www.selahpub.com. Used by permission. License no. 24131.

Excerpts from *WALTER HILTON: The Scale of Perfection*, from the Classics of Western Spirituality, translated from the Middle English, with an Introduction and Notes by John P. H. Clark and Rosemary Dorward, Copyright © 1991 by John P. H. Clark and Rosemary Dorward, Paulist Press, Inc., New York/Mahwah, N.J. Used with permission. www.paulistpress.com

Excerpts from *Hymns for Prayer and Praise* © 1996, The Panel of Monastic Musicians. Administered by SCM-Canterbury Press Ltd, Norwich NR3 3BH, England. Used by permission.

Fortem virile pectore by Silvio Antoniano. Text translated by Roger Nachtwey. © 1964 F.E.L. Assigned 1991 to The Lorenz Corporation. All rights reserved.

Rex gloriose martyrum © 1971 John Webster Grant.

About the Editor

William G. Storey is professor emeritus of Liturgy and Church History at the University of Notre Dame. He has compiled, edited, and authored some of the best-loved prayer books of our time, most notably *Lord, Hear Our Prayer; Hail Mary: A Marian Book of Hours; An Everyday Book of Hours; Mother of the Americas;* and *A Prayer Book of Catholic Devotions: Praying the Seasons and Feasts of the Church Year.* He currently resides in South Bend, Indiana.